Humility: Solidarity of the Humiliated

Humility:
Solidarity of the Humiliated

The transformation of an attitude and
its social relevance in Graeco-Roman,
Old Testament-Jewish and
Early Christian tradition

KLAUS WENGST

Fortress Press   Philadelphia

Translated by John Bowden from the German
Demut-Solidarität der Gedemütigten,
first published 1987 by Christian Kaiser Verlag, Munich.

© Christian Kaiser Verlag 1987

Translation © John Bowden 1988

First Fortress Press edition 1988

Library of Congress Cataloging-in-Publication Data

Wengst, Klaus.
  Humility: solidarity of the humiliated.

  Translation of: Demut, Solidarität der Gedemütigten.
  Bibliography: p.
  Includes index.
  I. Humility—History of doctrines.   I. Title.
  BV4647.H8W4613   1988   179′.9   88–45252

  ISBN 0–8006–2320–7

3445E88   Printed in the United Kingdom   1–2320

For Antonio Reiser

Contents

Preface

How does an author arrive at a topic for a book? This time I needed a series of promptings. Until not very long ago I would have thought it impossible that I would ever write about 'humility'. Similarly, friends looked at me in amazement when during the last two years I told them what I was working on. The first prompting, which to begin with got nowhere, came from Antonio Reiser, who argued that the poor and humble in the Beatitudes in Matthew were the *impoverished* and the *humiliated*. Before he returned to Argentina, during the period of his exile in West Germany he had several times given individual lectures within my lecture courses from which I gratefully learned a good deal. So this short book is dedicated to him. The second prompting came from a sermon I had to give on Ephesians 4.1-6. While I was preparing for it, it occurred to me that it could be exciting to work more intensively on the topic of humility. Further prompting was necessary for that in fact to happen: the *Festschrift* for the eightieth birthday of Professor Heinrich Greeven, the doyen of our faculty. Since my contribution got longer and longer as I worked it out, only part of it could be published in the *Festschrift*, the section on Paul and the Pauline tradition (it appears in *Studien zum Text und zur Ethik des Neuen Testaments*, ed. Wolfgang Schrage, BZNW 47, Berlin and New York 1986, 428-39). Since then I have worked over the whole passage again.

I am most grateful to Edith Lutz, who prepared the typescript and helped with work on investigating the non-biblical sources and in reading the proofs. For great help in the two latter tasks I am grateful to my students Karoline Hafer and Iris Lorenz, and for proof-reading also to my wife. My assistant Martin Leutzsch made more suggestions about the influence of the concept than I could use, and produced the index. My colleagues Gerhard Binder and Bernd Effe read through the Graeco-Roman part and Jürgen Ebach an earlier form of the Old Testament-Jewish part. I am also grateful to them.

Bochum, July 1987

I

Introduction
'It is always the secure who are humble'

'The trodden worm curls up. This testifies to its caution. It thus reduces its chances of being trodden upon again. In the language of morality: Humility' (Friedrich Nietzsche, *The Twilight of the Idols*, Maxims and Missiles 31, *Complete Works*, Volume 16, London 1911, 5f.).

'The most brilliant exponent of the egoistic school, Nietzsche, with deadly and honourable logic, admitted that the philosophy of self-satisfaction led to looking down upon the weak, the cowardly, and the ignorant. Looking down on things may be a delightful experience, only there is nothing, from a mountain to a cabbage, that is really *seen* when it is seen from a balloon. The philosopher of the ego sees everything, no doubt, from a high and rarefied heaven; only he sees everything foreshortened or deformed' (G.K.Chesterton, 'A Defence of Humility', in *The Defendant*, London 1914, 135).

With these remarks Chesterton addressed the question of perspective. He refers them both simply and convincingly to a single instance and yet does so enigmatically: 'That the trees are high and the grasses short is a mere accident of our own foot-rules and our own stature. But to the spirit which has stripped off for a moment its own idle temporal standards the grass is an everlasting forest, with dragons for denizens, the stones of the road are as incredible mountains piled one upon the other' (136). 'Meanwhile, the sage whose faith is in magnitude and ambition is, like a giant, becoming larger and larger, which only means that the stars are becoming smaller and smaller. World after world falls from him into insignificance; the whole passionate and intricate life of common things becomes... lost to him...' (137).

This question of perspective should also be raised in connection with the understanding of the term 'humility' itself and any evaluation of it. 'It has often already been asserted that the Greek word ταπεινός ('humble') and its derivatives in secular Greek primarily have a negative connotation... In the Old Testament..., the Septuagint and the New Testament, by contrast, this group of words almost always appears only with a positive significance.'[1] This finding will be confirmed more than once in the following accounts. But Rehrl's explanation seems to me to call for a further question. Walter Grundmann comments that 'The different estimation of the word group ταπεινός in Greek literature and the Bible is governed by the different understanding of man. The Greek concept of free man leads to contempt for lack of freedom and subjection. This qualifies ταπεινός and derivates negatively. In Israel and post-exilic Judaism, however, man is controlled by God's action. Man must listen to God and obey Him, so that he can call himself God's servant.'[2] Hans Helmut Esser takes up this distinction as that between anthropocentric and theocentric pictures of humankind.[3] According to Albrecht Dihle, humility can arise as a virtue only 'where one understands human beings *per se* as lowly, as sinners asking for grace. In principle both Greeks and Romans scorn any attitude or gesture which amounts to a diminution of the value of personality.'[4] But is not this talk of human beings *per se* an abstraction which is made all too quickly? There can be no doubt that there are respects in which differences between human beings are irrelevant before God, so that one can indeed speak of 'humankind'. First of all, however, one has to ask about specific human beings, and that also means about different social conditions which are the living conditions of those who speak in the texts and about whom statements are made. That is all the more obvious in connection with the term 'humility', since 'in accordance with its original meaning' it is connected with 'social data and... (belongs in) the great historical dialectic of the relationship between master and slave'.[5] What is understood by humility and how it is evaluated depends on who attributes it to whom and in what social and political situation. I shall go on to investigate this.[6] Regardless of the fact that it is right in principle to say that in the Graeco-Roman world 'humility' has negative connotations, but that these connotations are positive in the Old Testament, Judaism and early Christianity, there are substantial shifts in the understanding of the term within individual spheres of tradition.[7]

Chesterton speaks of the 'visions of him who, like the child in the fairy tales, is not afraid to become small' (137).Not to be afraid to become small and therefore to have the vision of a community of people among whom there are no great ones who tread on the small like worms, and in which there are no small ones who have to dodge the great – such a line of humility could be drawn through the Old Testament-Jewish-primitive Christian tradition which we shall be recalling here. According to Chesterton people felt safe to whom 'a covenant[8] with God... opened up a clear deliverance... they believed themselves rich with an irrevocable benediction which set them above the stars; and immediately they discovered humility... It is always the secure who are humble' (134f.).

II

'Shameful deeds, lowly origin, sordid poverty and mean handiwork or trade.' 'Humility' in the Graeco-Roman tradition

'Humility as a virtue is alien to the whole of ancient ethics.'[1] However, we should look more closely to see from what perspective the concept of humility is shaped here. It is striking that among the authors of Greek and Roman antiquity the words which denote 'humble' and 'humility'[2] often appear in a clear social and political context. A decisive factor in understanding the terms is that those in high social positions use them to speak 'from above' about those in low social positions. The value of the concept of humility defined in this way usually also remains where it is detached from this context.

1. 'Nobodies like ourselves.' 'Humility' as a lowly social position

A relatively late piece of evidence, Aelius Aristides' eulogy of Rome, offers a primary meaning of the Greek term. Aristides is quoting a remark of Oibaras, who is said to have made clear to the Persian king in a metaphorical comparison why he had to travel round his kingdom: 'Let him see what happens to a hosepipe: the parts on which he treads are pressed down (ταπεινὰ ἐγίγνετο) and touch the earth, whereas the parts from which his foot is removed rise up again and are pressed down again (ἐταπεινοῦντο) only when he treads on them once more.'[3] According to this the 'humble' would be those who are oppressed and downtrodden by rule. Thus Caesar describes in 'what a humiliating situation' (*quam humiles*) he had found the Aedui: 'crowded into towns, deprived of fields, all their resources plundered, a tribute imposed, hostages wrung from them with the utmost insolence'.[4] Therefore it may appropriately be said: 'A person or a people or a state can be not just lowly and insignificant in itself, but can also be *made lowly*, e.g. through force of arms and the superior might of others.'[5] A very old piece of evidence confirms that in respect of individuals. In Euripides' *Andromache* Queen Hermione threatens Andromache, who has been made a slave, with death, and then continues:

> Yet though one stoop to save thee, man or god,
> Yet must thou for thy haughty spirit of old
> Crouch low abased, and grovel at my knee (πτῆξαι ταπεινήν),
> And sweep mine house, and sprinkle water dews
> There from the golden ewer with thine hand,
> and where thou art, know.[6]

The 'humble' woman here is the slave who has to fall on her knees before her mistress and perform the most menial duties. A passage in Seneca sounds more friendly when he calls slaves 'friends of lower status' (*humiles*).[7] At all events, it is clear that the term denotes a lowly social status. However, it is in no way limited to slaves but embraces by far the majority of the population. The *humiliores*, the lower classes, the 'lowly', are set over against a thin upper class.[8] They are the ordinary people, the *plebs*.[9] According to Cicero it should be noted that in legal defence, 'If one defends a man who is poor, but honest and upright, all the lowly (*humiles*) who are not dishonest – and there is a large proportion of the sort among the people – look upon such an advocate as a tower of defence raised up for them.'[10] Balbus and Oppius, Roman knights and officials of Caesar, make themselves more insignificant than they are when they write to Cicero: 'Advice – even the advice of distinguished persons, let alone nobodies (*hominum humilium*) like ourselves – is generally judged by results and not by intention.'[11]

2. 'With your back bent over your work... altogether humble.' 'Humility' as the lowly disposition of insignificant people

Seen from above, a lowly attitude goes with a lowly social position: the lowly position leads to a lowly disposition which expresses itself in flattery and insubordination. The slave also has a slave morality.[11a]

Thus in one passage Aristotle distinguishes between voluntary work and forced labour. The latter is given to the lowly craftsman (βάναυσος). 'A task and also an art or a science must be deemed vulgar if it renders the body or soul or mind of free men useless for the employment and actions of virtue (ἀρετή). Hence we entitle vulgar all such arts as deteriorate the condition of the body, and also the industries that earn wages, for they make the mind preoccupied and degraded (ταπεινήν).'[12] Similarly, Pliny asks a friend who is staying in Como: 'Why do you not delegate the lowly and dirty tasks (*humiles et sordidas curas*) to others – it is high time – and devote yourself in the deep, comfortable seclusion there to your studies?'[13] Lowly occupations and the bravery of the free man are mutually exclusive. Homer already remarks: 'When the masters no longer command, the slaves will no longer do their duties. Zeus takes away half the virtue of a man when he allows him to be made a slave.'[14] Only the free and independent person can have virtue (ἀρετή). Existence as a slave which is characterized by work imposed by another precludes real virtue, acting on one's own impulse. The 'lowly disposition', 'humility', is thus a matter of the 'subjection of the slave brought about by his social position'.[15] The nature of society at a particular time offers particular possibilities and also determines human consciousness. This recognition could only lead to the desire not to be turned into a slave.[16]

In the passages of Aristotle quoted above, lowly occupations which make people unfit in body, soul and thought include all strenuous physical labour and all paid work. The connection between social status and disposition is clearly expressed when it is said that such occupations demean thought. A distinction must be made between free and unfree, noble and common work. This contempt for manual work also appears in Livy, when he describes the origins of Terentius Varro not as lowly (*humilis*), but even as dirty (*sordidus*), and then continues: 'His father is said to have been a butcher who sold his own wares and trained his son to the servile practices of his trade.'[17] In another passage he reports that someone nominated for the Senate was accused of 'shameful deeds, lowly origin (*humilitas*), sordid poverty and mean handiwork or trade.'[18] We find the same sort of thing in Seneca. At one point he makes the objection: 'In teaching language, in the art of healing and in seafaring, we see that it is the lowliest (*humillimi*) who gain possessions.' He argues against this that these gains are not aimed at spiritual growth and then asserts: 'Anyone who is not a man of virtue (*vir bonus*) cannot become a doctor, a helmsman or a teacher of languages any more than he can become – by god! – a cook.'[19] If according to Aristotle the children of the free may be educated only in free work because those who are compelled to work also have a lowly disposition, Seneca describes the education of a boy like this: 'Let him not tolerate anything lowly (*humile*), anything servile; let it never be necessary for him to fall down on his knees, nor useful to have asked.'[20]

At another point Aristotle describes as 'too humble' (ταπεινοὶ λίαν) those who in an extreme form suffer lack of power, riches, influential friends and the like. Here 'humility' would be synonymous with poverty and lack of public influence. Anyone who is socially determined in this way cannot rule. He can only obey a rule which is exercised over slaves.[21] The counterpart of the lowly and the humble man is the high-minded man (μεγαλόψυχος). Aristotle also describes him in connection with his social status, when he says that among his qualities should be to need no one, or at any rate only to a very small degree, but to be ready to lend support and to measure himself by those in high positions.[22] He has in mind the self-sufficient person, of whom he said earlier: 'May we not then confidently pronounce that man happy who realizes complete virtue in action, and is adequately furnished with external goods?'[23] According to the previous passage this 'happy' person enters into laudable competition with his like. In the competitive society of the powerful a comparison with the lowly is felt to be almost unrespectable. It must therefore be avoided, just as it is also unseemly for the healthy to vaunt themselves before the sick. As this comparison between the healthy and the sick shows, social conditions are regarded as natural. That the sick are to be healed does not, however, become a simile in Aristotle. Social changes do not come within his horizon. He is writing for the better-off. He also commends mildness to them.[24] He does not use mildness and 'humility' in parallel, but he evaluates mildness in a positive way and 'humility' in a negative way, and attributes them to different groups of people. Mildness is furthered from above,[25] last of all also to those who humble themselves and thus demonstrate their inferiority: 'Men are also mild (πρᾶοι) towards those who humble themselves (τοῖς ταπεινουμένοις) before them and do not contradict them, for they seem to recognize that they are inferior. Now those who are inferior are afraid, and no one who is afraid slights another. Even the behaviour of dogs proves that anger ceases towards those who humble themselves, for they do not bite those who sit down.'[26] The competitive society is shaped by latent fear of one another. If the power relationships are clarified and a hierarchy is produced in the 'dog-pack society', on the one hand gentleness can prevail and on the other hand fear and 'humility' find a place.[27]

In Xenophon, too, we can see a connection between social position and ethical qualification. In a conversation with a painter about whether it is possible to paint the inner nature of a person, he makes Socrates produce a series of contrasts. On the one hand there are nobility, respectability (the nature of a free person: τὸ ἐλευθέριον), thoughtful and rational aspects like beautiful, good and lovable behaviour, and on the other lowliness/humility (τὸ ταπεινόν), meanness (the nature of

one who is not free: τὸ ἀνελεύθερον), arrogance and roughness, along
with bad, evil and hateful behaviour.[28]

Lucian provides the most illuminating text in this connection. He
tells how after his schooldays he had been sent to his uncle to be a
stonemason. On the very first day after his flight he had a dream in
which two women, one beautiful and one ugly, quarrelled over him.
Finally the decision was left to him, after each had introduced herself.
One, Education, commented on the promises of the other, Sculpture,
like this: 'What it shall profit you to become a sculptor, this woman has
told you: you will be nothing but a labourer, toiling with your body and
putting in it your entire hope of a livelihood, personally inconspicuous
(ταπεινὸς τὴν γνώμην), getting meagre and illiberal returns, humble-
witted, an insignificant figure in public, neither sought by your friends
nor envied by your fellow-citizens – nothing but just a labourer, one of
the swarming rabble, ever cringing to the man above you and courting
the man who can use his tongue, leading a dog's life, and counting as a
godsend to anyone stronger.'[29] At the end of her speech Education
describes to Lucian again what fate will await him if he devotes himself
to the art of sculpture: 'You will put on a filthy tunic, assume a servile
appearance, and hold bars and gravers and sledges and chisels in your
hands, with your back bent over your work. You will be a groundling,
with groundling ambitions, altogether humble (ταπεινός); you will
never lift your head, or conceive a single manly or liberal thought.'[30] It
is thought to be worth striving to be the envy of one's fellow-citizens,
to support friends before the judgment and to be able to instil fear into
one's enemies. The social model is that of the prosperous and influential
person. He looks down contemptuously on 'little people' who have to
earn their food laboriously with the work of their hands. Anyone who
is and remains in such a lowly position can only have a 'lowly disposition',
be 'humble'.[31]

3. 'All ways are open to all...' Upward social mobility as the way out of 'humility'

Lucian, a child of ordinary people, escapes his milieu and as an individual
looks for a possible 'way up'. He finds it in education with the help of
which he, 'the beggarly son of a nobody', can make contacts with a
better circle. In the dream Education promises him that he will be
'honoured and lauded, held in great esteem for the highest qualities,
even admired by men pre-eminent in lineage and in wealth, and will be
deemed worthy of office and precedence.'[32] If he devotes himself to her

he has the prospect of 'a dignified appearance, honour, esteem, praise, precedence, power and offices, upon fame for eloquence and felicitations for wit'.[33] Lucian took this course, and so he presents himself at the end of this short work as an example – he who despite his poverty at the time was not resigned, but has 'become something' through education. Therefore he has told his dream so 'that those who are young may take the better direction and cleave to education, above all if poverty is making any one of them faint-hearted and inclining him towards the worse, to the detriment of a noble nature'.[34]

Lucian is an example of the possibility of upward social mobility. Society at the time of the Roman empire had a stratified social structure in which the dividing line between upper class and lower class was particularly marked; origin, above all social, but also geographical origin, played a decisive role.[35] Yet the boundaries within the hierarchical social structure were in no way hermetically sealed against one another. In certain areas social mobility was relatively widespread. Thus the house slave in the city could hope to be freed around his thirtieth birthday.[36] The child of the freedman born after he received his freedom was already regarded as freeborn.[37] In addition to social downfall,[38] even before the time of the empire there were constant cases of considerable upward social mobility, and these became even more frequent during the empire.[39] Though the divisions within society were no longer taken for granted by many people,[40] there was a need for the possibility of upward social mobility and occasional instances of it – related to the total number of those living in the lower classes – in order to legitimate and thus also preserve the existing social structure.[41] It could then be suggested that anyone could improve his position by appropriate achievement. Thus Aelius Aristides stresses that there are no geographical barriers to 'being a Roman citizen'. 'All ways are open to all; no one is a stranger who proves worthy of an office or a place of trust. All stream as it were to a common market, each to get what is his due.'[42] With an eye to the military sphere Aelius Aristides praises the emperor for giving foreigners he had recruited the hope 'that they would not regret it if they proved to be brave men; for people from the old nobility would not always take first place nor people from the second class the second place, and even in the other ranks it would not be like this, but each would attain the rank that he deserved, as the brave would not be judged here by words but by deeds.'[43]

Despite all the differences, caused above all by the great significance of origins, the American legend of the rise from 'dish-washer to millionaire' offers a modern analogy. Even if there have in fact been such careers – and imperial Rome also had amazing careers to point out – they are 'legendary' in a particular sense of the word: they are spoken of as a dream which once came true, which supports them in the system and in fact remains for most people an unattainable possibility – as indeed it must, for how otherwise would the system exist? But as there is this possibility, however limited, popular opinion can regard those who do not achieve the rise as personal failures, and in this way disguise enslaving structures.

An awareness of the opportunity to rise was established in Rome as it were from the beginning. Livy relates that at his founding of the city Romulus acted in accordance with an 'age-old plan of those who founded cities, who gathered an unknown and lowly (*obscuram atque humilem*) crowd around them and made Rome a sanctuary'. 'Thither fled from the surrounding people a miscellaneous rabble, without distinction of bond or free, eager for new conditions; and these constituted the first advance in power.'[44] Thus in the history of Rome it was time and again the case that someone from lowly origins rose into a high (or even the highest) position.[45] According to Quintilian, 'fatherland, parents and ancestors' should be mentioned first in the praise of a man: 'For either it would be creditable to the objects of our praise not to have fallen short of the fair fame of their country and of their sires, or to have ennobled a humble origin (*humilius genus*) by the glory of their achievements.'[46]

If such a social rise is possible in principle, and individuals succeed 'getting on in the world', the awareness of upward social mobility becomes a widespread social phenomenon. Over against the 'lowly disposition', 'humility', there would be the 'lofty disposition', the attempt to get out of the milieu of the small people, the mentality of the social climber.

4. 'Should we say that Fortune makes men petty, timid, and abject in spirit?' The inner freedom of 'humility' in social decline

If the texts discussed in the previous section represented a close connection between lowly social status and lowly disposition, by contrast there is also the possibility that a person in a high position can have a lowly disposition. In that case he acts in a way which does not correspond with his status, as it were 'below his level'. Tacitus reports of a governor of Britain who in a mutiny 'eluded the violence of the soldiery by escaping to a hiding place', thus acting 'at the cost of shame and humiliation' (*indecorus atque humilis*).[47] Pliny assures a friend who is going to Achaea as a governor that he need not fear contempt if he avoids arrogance and harshness when exercising his office: 'Can he who is vested with the powers and bears the ensigns of the state - can he be contemned, unless he is a low, sordid being (*humilis atque sordidus*) and sets the example by his self-contempt?'[48] In another passage Pliny tells of an honour resolved on by the senate for Pallas, a freeman of the emperor Claudius. It was 'as if Caesar went to put up a notice of his weakness, the Senate of his servility (*humilitas*), and Pallas of his insolence, in the face of the world'.[49] The person in a high position can make himself 'mean'; even a king can. However, Dio Chrysostom's view is that Zeus does away with a king who is 'knavish, treacherous, degraded (ταπεινός), wilful'.[50] When he takes over as consul, in the speech in praise of Trajan which had to be given on this occasion Pliny makes this emperor the best possible *princeps* and compares with him the deficiencies of others: 'One man may have shone in war, but his glory has grown dim in time of peace, while another has distinguished himself in civil life but not in arms. Some have won respect through men's fear (*terror*), while others in courting popularity have sunk low (*humilitas*).'[51] Such *humilitas* is not in accordance with their status, and to be in accordance with one's status is in one of the essential norms in a society dominated by status.

So if it is possible for the person in a high position to remain humble in contrast to his status, it can be asked what effect this has on his behaviour if his situation changes and he goes down in the world. This possibility is often considered by Plutarch and answered clearly. First of all, however, it should be stressed that Plutarch, too, maintains the connection between lowly social status and lowly disposition. In a context in which he explains how admiration of a work can go along with contempt for the person who produces it,[52] he writes: 'Labour with one's hands in lowly tasks (ἡ αὐτουργία τῶν ταπεινῶν) gives witness, in the toil thus expended on useless things, to one's indifference to higher things.'[53] And at another point he argues: 'A goodly treasure, then, is honourable birth, and such a man may speak his mind freely, a thing which should be held of the highest account by those who wish to have issue lawfully begotten. In the nature of things the spirits of those whose blood is base or counterfeit are constantly being brought down and humbled' (ταπεινοῦσθαι).[54] Thus it is already clear that in Plutarch the contrasting of concepts and the evaluations made here are in no way different from his tradition. So he speaks of the 'boldness of vice', which, 'as the gale of passion dies away, falls a weak and abject prey (ἀσθενὴς καὶ ταπεινός) to terrors and superstitions.'[55] So he lists those who are 'insignificant, anxious and of a lowly disposition/humble' (ταπεινόφρων) one after the other and sums them up under 'meanness' (κακία), putting 'courage and intelligence' (ἀνδρεία καὶ φρόνησις) on the other side.[56] On the one hand are 'base, cowardly, lowly/humble (ταπεινόφρων), ignoble and envious', and on the other 'good, valiant, high-souled'.[57] It is regarded as 'in every respect useless, meaningless and senseless' to trouble oneself further and demean/humble oneself (ταπεινοῦν ἑαυτόν), once one gets into an undesirable situation.[58] Here too the free citizen with possessions, the strong citizen, is envisaged. He has bravery and courage, and has nothing to do with fearfulness, cowardice, meanness and humility.

Now if this citizen suffers a deterioration in his circumstances as a result of fate, that need not, Plutarch stresses, mean that his disposition changes. Whereas Homer had asserted that the free man loses half his virtue as soon as he is enslaved, Plutarch affirms the possibility of his keeping it. 'Should we say, then, that Fortune makes men petty, timid and abject in spirit? Yet it is not right for anyone to charge baseness to misfortune, or courage and intelligence to good fortune.'[59] 'Fortune, in fact, can encompass with sickness, take away our possessions, slander us to people or despot, but she cannot make the good and valiant and high-souled man base or cowardly, mean, ignoble or envious, nor can she deprive us of that disposition, the constant presence of which is more help in facing life than is a pilot in facing the sea.'[60] Also according to Plutarch, then, insignificant people have an 'abject spirit/humility'. He is only challenging the assumption that the more exalted free citizen will inevitably have a similar disposition when he gets into a comparable position.

Plutarch was a member of the Greek upper class which under the Roman provincial administration could have only limited political responsibility. The 'fate' that made the circumstances of members of his class worse will often enough have borne the name 'Rome' and taken the form of the proconsul.[61] Instances of social decline were probably far more numerous in his time than in the world of Homer. That is the specific social and political background to his assertion of the possibility of inner freedom against the 'blows of fate'.

5. 'Noble, high-minded and freeborn by nature.' The internalized individual and his freedom from 'humility'

Stoic tradition not only asserts the inner freedom of the well-to-do citizen, which means that he does not have to adopt a lowly disposition in the face of a blow of fate which oppresses him, but also regards men generally as inwardly free, so that they can also be free from 'humility'. That becomes particular clear from the remarks of Seneca and Epictetus.

Seneca, as rich as Croesus, thinks that 'Virtue is no smaller when it is reduced from prouder heights to a private station, from a royal palace to a humble dwelling, or when from a general and broad jurisdiction it is gathered into the narrow limits of a private house or tiny corner.'[62] He makes Socrates imagine on the one hand celebrating a triumph and on the other hand being taken along in the triumphal procession as a piece of plunder. Socrates then continues: 'No whit more humble (*humilior*) shall I be when I am driven in front of the chariot of another than when I stood erect upon my own.'[63] Therefore virtue can be looked on – provided that the perception of the soul is freed from hindrances – 'though it be buried in the body, even though poverty stand in the way, and even though lowliness (*humilitas*) and disgrace block the path'.[64] Virtue is not bound to external events: 'A great man can spring from a hovel; so can a beautiful and great soul from an insignificant (*humilis*) body. For this reason Nature seems to me to breed certain men of this stamp with the ideal of proving that virtue springs to birth in any place whatever.'[65]

Seneca relativizes what is important in the world from a loftier standpoint. The wise man who has become a citizen of the world and thus is as it were transported into heaven 'understands how lowly (*humilis*) was the place in which he sat when he mounted the curule chair or judgment seat'.[66] Within the world there takes place a relativization of fate to which all are subject. At the latest by now it can be seen that only a rich person can talk like this, one who is evidently unaware of the sheer cynicism which is emerging here. 'All of us are chained to fortune. Some are bound by a loose and golden chain, others by a tight chain of base metal: but what difference does it make? The same captivity holds all men in its toils... Some are chained by public office, others by wealth; some carry the burden of high birth, some of low birth (*humilitas*).' In short: 'All life is a servitude.'[67] The consequence of this is that 'a man must become reconciled to his lot';[68] and that also means: 'poverty is an evil to no man unless he kick against the goads'.[69] Seneca is not poor and he can value that. Certainly, the 'true good things are those which reason gives'; the rest have only the name in common, but they are 'advantages' and 'things to be preferred' if one has the choice, even if 'they are to be reckoned as things subordinate and poor (*humilia*)'.[70]

For the former slave Epictetus every man is 'a living being endowed with reason' (λογικὸν ζῷον).As such each man is 'by nature noble, high-minded and freeborn'.[71] The man defined by the gift of reason is not by nature bound by his social relationships. Therefore Epictetus completely detaches the ethical concepts of his tradition, which there had been bound to social status, from this social imprisonment and internalizes them. Real humanity is limited to the sphere of those things which the individual has in his hand no matter in what situation he finds himself, which he can freely choose and which are independent. If he holds to them, 'he will be free, serene, happy, unharmed, high-minded, reverent, giving thanks for all things to God, in no circumstances finding fault with anything that has happened, nor blaming anything'. On the other hand, 'he must needs be hindered and restrained, be a slave to those who have control over those things which he has admired and feared; he must needs be irreverent, for as much as he thinks that God is injuring him, and be unfair, always trying to secure for himself more than his share, and must needs be of an abject and mean spirit.'[72] Epictetus mentions as things which the person has in his hand 'being right in judgment, in thinking, in choosing, in desiring,in avoiding. Where is there any longer room for flattery, where for an abject spirit (ταπεινοφροσύνη)?'[73] What lies outside the things mentioned here is irrelevant. That is the price Epictetus pays for taking over the value system of a hierarchical society and seeking to make it apply to everyone in the same way. So he has to strip the specific individual of his social qualities in order to arrive at *the* human being, an abstract theoretical construct. He can claim the values that he has taken over only for the completely internalized individual who is not affected by anything outside the things that have been mentioned.

Excursus: The positive use of 'humility'

'Humility' is used positively in only a very few passages of ancient literature. Its context here is a man's attitude towards the gods. In discussing the problem that the punishment of the deity often affects the evildoer only at a very late stage, Plutarch makes his conversation partner produce a comparison with the trainer of a horse which only learns when it feels the punishing blow the moment it puts a foot wrong. He then continues: 'In like manner a viciousness that at every stumble and plunge is whipped and pulled up by punishment might at last become circumspect and humble (ταπεινή) and fearful of God as one who in his government of the affairs and passions of men is procrastinating justice.'[74] Only in this context of the punishing of the evildoer who is to be given a sense of wrongness are humility and fear given a positive significance.[75] That this does not amount to a positive evaluation of humility emerges when it is said rather earlier in the text that an absence of retribution 'weakens the cheated victim in his hopes and breaks his spirit' (ἀσθενή... ταῖς ἐλπίσιν ποιεῖ καὶ ταπεινὸν τὸν ἀδικούμενον).[76] Statius speaks at one point of changing the mind of the gods 'by humble (*humilis*) petition'.[77] Propertius begins an elegy with the lines 'Bacchus, we now bow humble (*humiles*) before your altar'[78] – and in so doing has drinking wine in mind.

So 'humility' is used in a positive sense when it is meant to describe the deliberate modesty of a life-style free from conceit and the quest for fame. Thus Dio Chrysostom speaks of the 'man who is noble, thoughtful and moderate', who does not long for riches and praise. 'He will go through life as simply as possible and without conceit, modest (ταπεινός) and moderate in himself and in his own consciousness.'[79] Propertius speaks in such a way of his patron Maecenas: 'You exercise renunciation and withdraw modestly (*humilis*) into the scanty shade.'[80]

In this contrast with arrogance, 'humility' can be attributed even to kings as a positive property. Thus in Xenophon's *Agesilaos* it is said of this king that he was not arrogant, 'but rather despised the overweeningly proud and was more modest (ταπεινότερος) than ordinary people', with no personal needs and generous to strangers.[81] The *Historia Augusta* reports of Julian: 'He was also accused of conceit, though even when exercising rule he had shown himself to be very modest (*humillimus*).'[82]

Finally Propertius commends humility to his beloved as a better way of achieving an end: 'Yet the more modest (*humilis*) you are and subservient to love, the more you will have the success you desire.'[83]

III

'Thou art the God who humblest thyself.'
God's partiality in the
Old Testament-Jewish tradition

'Humility' is not spoken of in the Old Testament and in Judaism in at all the same way as in the Greek and Roman sphere. Here, too, a connection is seen with social reality, but the perspective of the perception is completely different. Whereas in the Greek and Latin texts ordinary people are looked down on from above, so that they appear 'common, mean, subservient, humble', the Old Testament texts speak from the perspective of these insignificant people and take the side of those who are exposed to being downtrodden and to humiliation. If in the Greek sphere there is a tendency to detach the negative concept from its social roots, so that the person affected by social downfall need not necessarily be associated with it, and indeed in principle anyone can be free of it, in the Old Testament and Jewish sphere there is a similar tendency which allows the term with a positive content also to be applied to the rich.

1. 'They trample the head of the poor into the dust of the earth.' Poverty as humiliation

(a) Just as in Greek and Latin texts 'humility' can characterize social status as being lowly, the same is true in the Hebrew Bible of similar terms which in the Septuagint are translated with forms based on the root ταπεινο-. In Amos 2.6f. the prophet cites as a word of God: 'For three transgressions of Israel, and for four, I will not revoke the punishment; because they sell the righteous because of silver, and the needy (*'ebyōn*/πένης) because of[1] a pair of shoes. They trample the head of the poor (*dallīm*/πτωχοί) into the dust of the earth, and turn aside the way of the afflicted (*'anāwīm*/ταπεινοί).' What kind of circumstances are presupposed here and what procedures are meant?

Amos emerged in the northern kingdom of Israel at the time of Jeroboam II (787-747 BC),[2] who as a result of military successes had been able to restore his frontiers to approximately those of the northern half of the kingdom of David and Solomon.[3] Safety from external enemies was matched within the kingdom by a so-called economic boom,[4] which produced a powerful 'social upheaval'.[5]

This economic development was to the advantage of the upper classes living in the city.[6] The luxurious life of the rich is clearly brought out by Amos; they have winter houses and summer houses (3.15a), built in modern and expensive quarried stone (5.11), adorned with ivory (3.15b) and decked out with fine interiors (3.12b; 6.4a), and they enjoy a particularly cultivated life-style with choice foods (6.4b), abundant wine (6.6a), music and song (6.5), and cosmetics (6.6b).[7]

On the other hand there is social decline: smallholders find themselves in increasingly more oppressive dependence.[8] Because of frequent crop failures or because of 'illness, paying dowries and the like'[9] they are compelled to take credit, and sooner or later become tenants who have to hand over what they produce (2.8; 5.11).[10] When the debts get more than the tenants can pay, all that is left is for them to be sold into slavery for debt. In 8.5f. Amos makes rich grain merchants say: 'When will the new moon be over, that we may sell grain? And the sabbath that we may offer wheat for sale, that we may make the ephah small and the shekel great, and deal deceitfully with false balances, that we may buy the poor because of money (debts) and the needy because of a pair of sandals, and sell the refuse of the wheat.' What is at first an enigmatic mention of sandals, which is often interpreted in terms of the insignificance of the debt,[11] is best explained by assuming that 'the transferred meaning "treaty" here in Amos also has the connotation "treaty of debt"'.[12] The rich 'buy' the poor, by bringing them into slavery for debt through deliberate manipulation and thus make them completely dependent.[13] The text in 2.6 which I cited at the beginning represents yet a further development here when it speaks of selling the righteous and the poor; this is probably a reference to selling the slave abroad, preventing any future return.[14]

Even if the law is secretly manipulated,[15] the actions of the rich do take place formally within the framework of the existing law.[16] Those who fall from being free farmers to tenants and are enslaved to debt or even sold abroad as slaves are not 'without debt, but owe an abundance of offerings'.[17]

In Isa.29.20f.,[18] which probably belongs to a very much later period, the parallel to the violent (*'ārīṣ/ἄνομος*) and the arrogant (*lēṣ/ὑπερήφανος*) are those who 'watch to do evil, who by a word make a man out to be an offender, and lay a snare for him who reproves in the gate, and with an empty plea turn aside him who is in the right'. Thus the people envisaged here attempt through bribery, intimidation, compulsion and deliberate perjury to make the law serve them and their interests. So these are people who 'are primarily to be sought in circles which can exercise political and economic pressure'.[19] If such procedures are successful, they result not only in gain for those who practise them but on the other hand in those humble/ lowly (*'aṇāwīm/πτωχοί*) and poor (*'ebyōnīm/ἀπηλπισμένοι*) and poor mentioned earlier in Isa.29.19, to whom God's promise applies.

Amos now demonstrates as clearly as one could wish that the riches of some, their extravagant and sybaritic life, rests on the exploitation and thus the distress and misery of the others (2.8; 4.1; 8.5f.).[20] What the rich are doing, very skilfully and very deliberately, is quite simply engaging in class warfare from above.[21] Their economic action, by means of which they seek to increase their wealth and also in fact become richer, intensifies the social conflicts among the people and makes others poorer. When Amos speaks of the 'poor' in such a context, which he perceives very clearly, it would be more accurate to translate the term he uses as 'impoverished', to make it clear that he is not describing a static situation but the result of a process initiated and carried on by human beings. So it would be more accurate to translate the text of Amos 2.6f. which I quoted at the beginning: 'For three transgressions of Israel, and for four, I will not revoke the punishment; because they sell the righteous because of money (debts), and the impoverished because of a pair of sandals. They trample the head of those who have been distressed into the dust of the earth, and turn aside the way of the afflicted/humiliated.'[22]

Where does Amos stand in this confrontation? It is impossible to draw any firm conclusion from the information about his profession in 1.1; 7.14f. about his social status. According to that passage he was a shepherd looking after sheep and goats; he may have bred them and even owned them; and he was a 'preparer of sycamore figs'. Regardless of what we are to understand by that, he cannot have carried on this profession in Tekoa, which is given as his home, since sycamores 'do not flourish in the hill-country of Judaea, but in the still accessible remoteness of the depths of the Jordan valley and on the coastal plain by the Mediterranean'.[23] So for this work he travelled round the country. He himself was not one of those immediately affected by exploitation and could evidently afford to function as a 'free prophet', someone who knows that he is far from being a professional prophet or a member of a prophetic association, and instead of this stresses his calling (7.14).[24] On the other hand Amos was certainly not a member of the upper classes resident in the cities, those whom he attacks.[25] He comes from Tekoa, a small place,[26] and his perspective is that of the countryman.[27] So he comes to see the damage done by social developments and condemns the wealth of the cities as an evil luxury, which is based on exploitation. Regardless of his social origin and position, Amos speaks on behalf of those who are forced out in the process of oppression[28] and with sharp analysis, accusation and threats attacks those who initiated this process and are carrying it on.

Now the most distinctive feature is that Amos does not present what he has to say as his own, but as God's word. He makes God discover the abuses, accuse and threaten. So in prophetic social criticism God is involved *a priori* from the beginning. Conditions evidently cry out to heaven to such a degree that change is only to be hoped for from heavenly intervention. In this way God appears unambiguously as an opponent of the rich upper classes and as an advocate of the impoverished and humiliated.

A very much later text expresses this preference on the part of God in a very fine way. The prayer of Judith in Judith 9.11 reads: 'For thy power depends not upon numbers, nor thy might upon men of strength; for thou art God of the lowly ($\tau\alpha\pi\epsilon\iota\nuo\iota$), helper of the insignificant ($\epsilon\lambda\alpha\tau\tauo\nuo\iota$), upholder of the weak ($\dot{\alpha}\sigma\theta\epsilon\nuo\hat{\upsilon}\nu\tau\epsilon\varsigma$), protector of the forlorn ($\dot{\alpha}\pi\epsilon\gamma\nu\omega\sigma\mu\epsilon\nuo\iota$), saviour of those without hope ($\dot{\alpha}\pi\eta\lambda\pi\iota\sigma\mu\epsilon\nuo\iota$).'[29]

What is the legal justification for this partisan word of God? How does Amos come to speak in this way? Who is the God understood in this way here? He is the God who brought Israel out of Egypt (2.10; 3.1; 9.7) and led them in the wilderness (2.10). He destroyed the Amorites, a great and mighty people, and thus made room for the weak Israel to live (2.9f.). The reference to the weakness of Jacob makes God twice repent of judgments which he has already resolved on (7.1-6).[30] As creator and governor of the universe God is at the same time the one who makes the strong and the fortified city perish (5.8f.). Because of the doings of the rich the earth must quake (8.8), and God makes it quake (9.5f.). Because God has 'known' Israel alone of all peoples, he will also visit its evil upon it (3.2). The election of Israel evidently calls for solidarity within the people. The formation of classes goes against the election. 'The crime of Joseph' (6.4-6) manifests itself in the life of luxury led by the rich.

Amos announces the destruction of the life of luxury (3.15; 4.2f.; 5.11f.; 6.7, 11) and holds out for the rich upper classes the prospect that they will have the experience of those whom they are now oppressing (2.14-16). His explicit announcement expresses nothing but a radical criticism of the existing order, i.e. the contrast between the rich cities and the land that they are draining. The judgment affects the cities.[31] But in that case is not the implication here the positive aim of a purposely egalitarian society in a land which is free from exploitation?[32]

In 2.6 and 5.12 we find 'the righteous' as a parallel term to other terms which denote the oppressed in society. 'Justice and righteousness' (5.7, 24; 6.12) are the exact opposite to what the rich upper classes are doing; 'what is straight', what is immediately due and needful and also right, is contrasted with violence and oppression (3.10). The one who is impoverished and distressed would thus at the same time be the righteous one in so far as he not only cannot use the violent means of the powerful but does not even strive for them, because he does not have the same aim, namely to become rich at the expense of others. Here there is an indication of how the one who has been socially 'humiliated' may become ethically 'humble'. We shall come back to that.

(*b*) The terminology of Amos 2.6f. and other passages I have mentioned also occurs in Isa.11.3b-5. The contrast of social groups explicitly made here allows us to argue for a similar social contrast to that seen by Amos. Isaiah looks to the coming messiah to overcome it, and describes him in his imagery as 'a shoot from the stump of Jesse' (11.1). Now that means that he in no way relies on the king who is actually reigning and his possible descendants, but rather assumes that the end of this dynastic line is already certain and hopes for the messiah from another line of the house of David.[33] The ruling king is evidently not doing at all what Isaiah expects of the coming messiah:[34] 'He shall not judge by what his eyes see, or decide by what his ears hear; but with righteousness he shall judge the impoverished (*dallīm*/ταπεινός), and decide with equity for the meek ('*nāwīm*/ταπεινοί) of the land; and he shall smite the evildoers[35] with the rod of his mouth and with the breath of his lips he shall slay the wicked (*rāšā'*/ἀσεβής). Righteousness shall be the girdle of his waist, and faithfulness the girdle of his loins.'[36]

Isaiah, the prominent citizen of Jerusalem, though in his perception and in what he says he does not allow himself to be influenced by the interest of his class, can only imagine the administration of justice as being carried out by the king. However, the royal messiah whom he announces adopts the perspective of the oppressed. He does not go by what he sees, which is determined by the strong, nor by popular opinion, which is directed by the powerful. Rather, he discloses the reality which is veiled and obscured by deception and manipulation and shows that the actual situation which is claimed to be just is in fact unjust. The messiah will help those who have no rights and those who have been humiliated to secure justice, the other side of which is action against the strong and powerful,[37] whose deeds are described as wicked.[38]

The place from which the messiah perceives reality is evidently below. Therefore he does not allow himself to be blinded by the splendour of economic prosperity nor will he be misled by the litanies of justification expressed by public opinion. From his perspective the situation of the poor does not appear as an unavoidable destiny but is recognized as impoverishment and lack of rights, as oppression and humiliation, which must be reversed.[39] A society which forces human beings to the margin, which produces those who are impoverished and humiliated, rests on evil power and is not the society that God wants.

The society intended in this text is not a competitive society divided into classes, and so there can be no question for someone in a lowly social position of seeking 'the way up'. The text outlines the picture of a society in which righteousness and trustworthiness prevail, the picture of a community in solidarity. Thus from the situation of humiliation the virtue of humility could arise if this situation is deliberately accepted in such a way that the humiliated themselves renounce humiliation and act in solidarity.

2. '... keep far away from their acts of violence!' The interruption of violence as the 'humility' of the poor

A series of further texts clearly shows a connection between riches, power and injustice on the one hand and connection between lowly social status and laudable ethical conduct on the other.

(*a*) The humiliated behave humbly in seeking refuge with God and not engaging in the unjust actions of those who use violence. This is stressed explicitly in Zeph.3.11b-13:[40] 'Then I will remove from your midst your proudly exultant ones, and you shall no longer be haughty in my holy mountain. For I will leave in the midst of you a people humble and lowly (*'ānī wādāl*/πραῦς καὶ ταπεινός). They shall seek refuge in the name of Yahweh, those who are left in Israel; they shall do no wrong and utter no lies, nor shall there be found in their mouth a deceitful tongue.' As the characterization of them as 'humble and lowly' shows, the people of God who are left are at the opposite social

extreme from the 'big Hanses',[41] 'that godless upper class'.[42] With its
translation πραΰς καὶ ταπεινός, here too the Septuagint already gives
social colouring to the ethical characterization.[43]

From the connection between social determination and ethical
conduct that has been observed, Zeph 2.3 might perhaps be translated
in a pointed way like this: 'Seek Yahweh, all you who have been
humiliated (*ᵃnāwē*/ταπεινοί) in the land, who do his commands; seek
righteousness, seek humility (*ᵃnāwā*).' The experience of humiliation
makes people cry out for righteousness. The humiliated are to seek
righteousness in such a way as to hold on to God's justice and not copy
the humble. In doing this they accept their situation of humiliation; and
this leads to humility as the solidarity of the humiliated.[44]

(*b*) Psalm 37[45] uses what is certainly traditional terminology.
However, in contrasting the two groups mentioned here, in describing
the actions of the one and the experiences of suffering by the others, in
the threats and promises which are produced, it indicates specific social
controversies. As the wisdom tradition[46] and the artificial form of the
psalm[47] suggest, the intellectual author is not himself one of the
disadvantaged. But he does speak on their behalf.

On the one hand are people who are described with negative
stereotypes. They are 'the wicked' (vv.1,9), 'the evildoers' (v.1), 'the
enemies of Yahweh' (v.20), 'those who curse him' (v.22), 'the apostates'
(v.38), and above all 'the wicked'.[48] At one point the wicked man is
explicitly called violent (v.35). So he obviously also has power. He is
one who 'imposes his way' and does so, as the parallel sentence shows,
with impure means: 'he plans evil devices' (v.7). These 'evil devices'
extend from threats to murder (vv.12, 14, 32). In this way riches are
generated (v.16b). The violent evildoer 'towers like a cedar of Lebanon'
(v.35). To dispense with metaphor: by unscrupulous use of all means
of power the rich increase their riches at the expense of the weaker
members of society.

In the threats made against them in this psalm they are again and
again virtually promised that they will perish. They will no longer exist;
their power will be broken.[49] They will have to borrow and will not be
able to repay (v.21a) – something quite outside their experience, though
it is the tormenting experience of those who are oppressed by them. This
is a mark of the social situation presupposed, which is the dependence of
poor smallholders on rich financiers.

The statements about those who stand over against the 'wicked'
underline that. They have few possessions (v.16a). They know 'bad
times' and 'days of hunger' (v.19; cf. v.39). They evidently have every

reason for anger and rage against the powerful in society (vv.1,7f.) to whose actions they are handed over (v.20), and therefore are threatened with such misery that it could compel them to make their children beg for their daily bread (v.25).

The promises given to them also clarify this situation. No fewer than five times it is stressed that they will possess the land.[50] The passage may have in mind those who have lost all or part of their land, who have been expelled from their holdings. Parallel to the promise of the land is that of the 'eternal heritage' (v.18) and permanent dwelling-place (v.27b). Shortly after that the two are precisely associated: 'The righteous shall possess the land, and dwell upon it for ever' (v.29).

That is at the same time a hope which goes against reality as it is experienced; for in fact the land is plundered by the poweful. A hope contrary to bad experiences is also depicted in vv.19-21a: 'They (viz. the righteous and the innocent) are not put to shame in evil times; in the days of famine they have abundance. But the wicked perish; the enemies of Yahweh are like the glory of the pastures; they vanish – like smoke they vanish away. The wicked borrow, but cannot pay back.' The very experience of the righteous in economic distress is that he does not have enough to satisfy the hunger of his family. He has to borrow and pay exorbitant interest. That drives him into even greater debt. He gets even poorer, whereas his harsh creditor makes profits.

The statement in v.25, in which the author of the psalm says, 'I have been young, and now am old, yet I have not seen the righteous forsaken or his children begging bread', must also be understood as a picture of hope against reality as it is experienced. In view of what the psalm says, even in explicit terms, about harsh reality which is so different, this sentence cannot be meant as naive description; it seems so overdrawn in this context that it can only be regarded as a contradiction of reality. It is not a postulate of the unspoilt world which is imagined by closing one's eyes to the real world but a contrast between the world willed by God and the actual chaos caused by humankind.[51]

The reality of God is constantly set against the power of the facts. The stress that God does not forsake those oppressed by the 'wicked' (vv.25,28) may suggest that their situation gives the impression that they have been abandoned by God. But, the psalm affirms, God supports them and saves them (vv.17, 39f.), as it were holds them by the hand (v.23f.). In the face of the actual situation, with 'the righteous' in the power of 'the wicked', we are told, 'but Yahweh will not abandon him to his power' (v.33a); and in the face of the *de facto* justice according to which the courts pronounce 'the righteous' guilty, so that he becomes the prey of 'the evil one', we are further told: 'and (Yahweh) will not let him (the righteous) be condemned when he (viz. the evil one) takes him (viz. the righteous one) to trial' (v.33b). The justice that God loves is contrasted with justice which is made an instrument to serve the powerful.

The assurance to the oppressed that against all appearances God is still on their side and not on the side of their oppressors, who are proving so successful, is meant to strengthen them to put their trust completely and utterly in God. The admonition made most often, to trust in God, to wait patiently for him and hope in him,[52] is certainly very traditional, but in the context of the psalm it takes on an evocative profile. Verse 7 runs: 'Be still before Yahweh and wait patiently for him; fret not yourself over him who prospers in his way, over the man who carries out evil devices.' Those who in the face of these unscrupulous evil devices set their hope only on God will refrain from opposing the evildoer at this level, from devising counter-measures of the same kind. There is no question that these people can have every reason for anger and rage; indeed that is presupposed. But they are not to do such things, so that they are not drawn into the same injustice: 'Refrain from anger and forsake wrath! Fret not yourself, it tends only to evil' (v.8). Hope in God makes the situation tolerable, and it allows alternatives to be developed: 'The righteous is generous and giving' (v.21b: cf. v.26a). So the possibility of sharing arises as opposed to lending against interest.

Given this, it is not surprising that both social and ethical terms are used to describe those who stand over against the evil doers. They are 'the poor and the impoverished' (v.14: *'ānī wĕ'ebyōnīm*/πτωχὸς καὶ πένης), 'those abased/humiliated/humble' (v.11: *'ănāwīm*/πραεῖς). They are at the same time described as 'pious' (v.28: *hᵃsīdīm*/ὅσιοι), 'innocent' (v.18: *tᵉmīmīm*/ἄμωμοι) and above all as 'righteous'[53] (*ṣaddīqīm*/δίκαιοι), as those who walk in the right way (v.14: *yišrē-derek*/οἱ εὐθεῖς τῇ καρδίᾳ). In this context the social terms have also taken on an ethical dimension. That might apply above all to 'humiliated, humble' (v.11: *'ănāwīm*).[54] At all events the Septuagint understood the term ethically, as is shown by the way in which it is translated οἱ πραεῖς ('the meek, gentle'). Those who have been humiliated and brought low show themelves to be humble and gentle by not attempting to imitate the actions of the evildoers (v.7). They are not resigned, but rely on the God who promises change and break out of the circle of violence in their relationship with one another. So the psalm is an offer of identification to the lowly, those who are oppressed and put at a disadvantage in social conflict. It gives them hope that their different form of behaviour will also benefit them, that those who praise God in this way will possess the land (v.22a) and will be able to make a living by tilling it, and that the violence of the evildoers will rebound on their own heads (v.22b).[55]

When the oppressed, down-trodden, and overpowered say to themselves with the vindictive guile of weakness, 'Let us be otherwise than the evil, namely, good! and good is everyone who does not oppress, who does not pay back, who hands over revenge to God, who holds himself, as we do, in hiding; who goes out of the way of evil, and demands, in short, little from life; like ourselves the patient, the meek, the just,' – yet all this, in its cold and unprejudiced interpretation, means nothing more than 'once for all, the weak are weak; it is good to do *nothing for which we are not strong enough*'; but this dismal state of affairs, this prudence of the lowest order, which even insects possess (which in a great danger are fain to sham death so as to avoid doing 'too much'), has, thanks to the counterfeiting and self-deception of weakness, come to masquerade in the pomp of an ascetic, mute, and expectant virtue, just as though the *very* weakness of the weak – that is, forsooth, its *being*, its working, its whole unique inevitable inseparable reality – were a voluntary result, something wished, chosen, a deed, an act of *merit*. This kind of man finds the belief in a neutral, free-choosing 'subject' *necessary* from an instinct of self-preservation, of self-assertion, in which every lie is fain to sanctify itself. The subject (or, to use popular language, the *soul*) has perhaps proved itself the best dogma in the world simply because it rendered possible to the horde of mortal, weak, and oppressed individuals of every kind, that most sublime specimen of self-deception, the interpretation of weakness as freedom, of being this, or being that, a *merit* (Friedrich Nietzsche, *The Genealogy of Morals*, Complete Works 13, London 1910, 46f.).

(c) The second part of the 'epistle of Enoch' (Ethiopian Enoch 94.6-104.13) is in the tradition of the texts discussed so far.[56] The world as the author perceives it is 'a world in disorder, a world of unresolved tensions and polar oppositions. Righteousness is out for the count.'[57] Two groups of people are opposed here: on the one side those who are marked out by riches and power, and on the other those who suffer under them and fight for sheer survival. The author is speaking from the perspective of the oppressed; he understands his role in analogy to that of the old prophets.[58]

Thus cries of woe are hurled at the rich and powerful in which their actions are castigated. Here, of course, we also often find traditional accusations of a general kind like those of injustice, unrighteousness and wickedness. But alongside them there are also statements which give us some very clear indications of the situation presupposed. Some clearly characterize the exploitative character of the actions of the powerful rich: 'Woe unto you who build your houses through the hard toil of others; and your building materials are bricks and stones of sin' (99.13).[59] The social contrast between the well-to-do free men on the one hand and the slaves and day-workers who depend on them on the other is seen to be a relationship of violence and is described as sinful. Riches obtained in such a relationship can only be described as 'acquired unjustly' (97.10). The enjoyment of some and the oppression of others match like two sides of the same coin: 'Woe to you who eat the best bread! And drink wine in large bowls,[60] trampling upon the weak people with your might!' (96.5).[61]

Here, too, oppression and exploitation have the semblance of justice. In 100.10 the reason given for the divine investigation of the sins of the rich is 'because you exercise judgment on the righteous on earth'. This charge might both apply to the fact that justice generally, because applied by the rich, serves their interests without the need for any formal legal offence, and also envisage unjust actions with which the rich unscrupulously break the law, which in any case favours them. One example of the latter is 99.12; 'Woe unto you who make sinful and deceitful measures!' As the continuation – 'and cause bitterness on earth' – indicates, when the rich deal with false measures and weights they need not particularly fear the discovery of such goings-on; the result will merely be to embitter the small people, who cannot do anything about it.

The charges against the rich, 'which more specifically relate to "religious" sins',[62] are closely connected with the socio-economic sphere. The focus here is on commandments which aim at a clear separation from the Gentile world. But such a separation gets in the way of business dealings with the Gentile world and may therefore often have been abandoned in the interest of encouraging trade. 'Woe to you who reject the foundations and the eternal inheritance of your fathers and who pursue the spirit of the abomination of idols' (99.14). Charges of eating blood,[63] blaspheming[64] and practising idolatry[65] could envisage specific meals with Gentile business partners in which the Jewish participants do not take offence at either the food (blood) or the place ('temple restaurant'). Their worldly liberality allows them to go beyond the narrow limits of their tradition.

Summing up, the author describes their actions in 102.9 as 'eating, drinking, robbing, sinning, casting people out naked (impoverishing them),[66] gaining property and seeing good days'.[67] From the perspective of the rich that can also be described and evaluated very differently:

their situation of being able to see good days and living to the full is a visible indication that the blessing of God rests on them. Thus the author says in 96.4, 'Your money makes you appear like the righteous.'[68] They have gained possessions because they were capable. What can they do if the other person has got into debt? He was probably lazy.[69] Over against this it should be stressed once again that the author sees the social situation as structural violence and describes it as sin.

How the situation looks to the oppressed is described most impressively in 103.9-15. This is a speech attributed to the 'righteous and good'. The author says that they should not talk like this. He does not forbid it because the content of what they say is inappropriate, but because there is more to say, because the promises which he adds in 104.1-6 apply. But they could speak like this; the description of the situation is quite accurate:[70]

> (9) In the days of our toil, we have surely suffered hardships and have experienced every trouble. We have faced many evil things and have become consumed. We have died and become few, characterized by the littleness of our spirit. (10) We have been destroyed; and we have found none whatsoever to help us with a word or otherwise. We have been tortured and destroyed, and could not even hope to see life from one day to the other. (11) We hoped to be the head and have become the tail. We have moiled as we toiled, but had no authority over our own toil. We have become the victuals of the sinners and the oppressors; they have made their yoke heavy upon us. Those who hate us, while goading us and encompassing us, have become masters over us. (12) We have bowed our necks to those who hate us, but they had no pity on us. (13) We wanted to get away from them in order to be safe from them. (14) Then, in our tribulation, we brought a charge against them before the authorities, and cried out against those who were devouring us, but the authorities neither would pay attention to our cries nor wished to listen to our voice. (15) But they were assisting those who were robbing and devouring us, those who were causing us to diminish. They conceal their injustice and do not remove the yokes of those who devour us, scatter us and murder us; they cover up our murder; and they do not remember that they (the oppressors) have lifted up their hand against us.[71]

The life of those who are speaking here is shaped by hard physical labour, which nevertheless does not bring them out of distress. On the contrary, they are constantly living a borderline existence: their bad living conditions are expressed in illness and a high mortality rate (9).[72]

Not even bare survival is ensured. They are exposed to trickery, deprived of their rights, and no one gives a penny for their lives (10). Deuteronomy 28.13[73] promises those who obey God's commandments that they will be the head and not the tail, will come at the beginning and not at the end. But here the experience of those who keep the commandments is that of being the dregs (11a). Despite their hard work they do not succeed in improving their situation (11b) because they do not enjoy the fruit of their work; it is taken by others who exploit them, under whose 'yoke' they are (11a). Here 'yoke' denotes the rule which manifests itself in economic exploitation. This rule is gained by power and is maintained by power (12a). It compels subservience, but the gesture of humility does not evoke any mercy (12b).[74] In such a hopeless situation thoughts turn to flight, to finding 'rest' (13a). It is the wish of those who have been forced to work hard to no advantage finally to have rest.[75] But this possibility of escape is then seen to be impossible. Where are they to flee to? (13b). Conditions will be just the same everywhere else; it would be no different. They could join a band of robbers or go underground in the sub-culture of a large city and survive by being more evil than good – but neither of these are possibilities for a pious man. The situation is really quite hopeless. A further possibility has also had to be ruled out: appeal to a higher political authority for intervention and help. The political authorities would not dream of acting against the interests of those with economic power. On the contrary, the authorities help them on, conceal and disguise their misdeeds and do not relieve the oppressed of their yoke (14f.).[76] For them the situation is hopeless on all sides. How can there be a way out here?[77]

The author discloses this situation by transcending it, by promising a future reversal. The houses of the rich will be destroyed (94.7); the rich will ooze out of their riches (94.8);[78] instead of peace (98.15; 99.13), rest (99.14) and a good life (99.1) they will have anxiety (98.3; 100.8) and be completely without hope for life (98.14), downtrodden on the earth (99.2). They will thus have the experiences of those who now oppress them.[79] This reversal is described particularly vividly in 98.12: 'Know that you shall be given over into the hands of the righteous ones.' Now the righteous ones are in the hands of those who oppress them and suffer mercilessly under them. But this situation is evidently so bad that it is not the slightest bit better to fall into the hands of the righteous, as the continuation of the text shows: 'And they shall cut off your necks and slay you, and they shall not have compassion on you.'[80] In the traditional way the righteous are often promised heavenly compensation.[81] One point should be noted particularly here. Their memory will not be blotted out (103.4); the angels in heaven are thinking of them and their names are written before God (104.1). Though they are worthless in public esteem, are quickly forgotten and no one thinks of them, they do have a place where they are thought of, where their name means something and where they have some worth. Over against the world of experience which gives cause for utmost resignation, the author proclaims as 'a revelation that things are not as they seem'.[82] Therefore he brings God into it. The situation is not just kept open by God in that he thinks of the oppressed and their names are written down before him. All the misdeeds of the powerful, too, are not forgotten but written down. It is argued against them that 'all your evil deeds are revealed in the heavens. None of your deeds of injustice are covered and hidden. Think not in your spirit, nor say in your hearts that you neither know nor see all your sins being written down every day in the presence of the Most High' (98.6-8). The angels and the sun, moon and stars, along with light and darkness, day and night, even cloud, dew and rain are made witnesses of this (100.10-13; 104.7f.). That which fears the light of day, which is deliberately swept away and is not meant to be made public (103.15), is hidden behind a massive veil of distorting propaganda (98.15),[83] namely the injustice of the powerful – that is unmistakeably manifest in heaven. To the extent that the apocalyptic author already participates in this heavenly publicity and similarly makes his readers participate in it, his writing and its circle of readers have an alternative public, legitimated by heaven, to the public dominated by the powers. Participation in the heavenly public already gives them the strength to call the action of the powerful rich what it is, namely unjust, and to remember it just as well as the names of their comrades in suffering who have perished or been killed, names which have been written in heaven.[84] The certainty that the injustice of the powerful is recorded by God therefore means more than that it can easily be forgotten and that God can be left to remember it. It becomes clear in 99.3 that it is rather a matter of not forgetting it oneself: 'In those days be ready, you righteous ones, to raise up your prayers as a memorial and place them as a testimony before the angels; and they (the angels) shall bring the sins of the sinners for a memorial before the Most High.' God's remembrance here serves as it were as a memorial of the oppressed righteous.[85] If they are to remember their prayers on the day of judgment they must have kept them in their thoughts. Prayer here becomes the medium of the alternative public.[86] It is to be expected that this alternative public will come up against attempts at intimation and pressures.[87] That explains not least the frequent admonition not to be afraid.[88] There is no question that here there is good reason to fear. And fear can lead to adaptation and compromise. This is clearest in 104.6. Here we can also see as the decisive motive behind the admonition not to be afraid: 'Do not be partners with them, but keep far away from their acts of violence.' And according to 102.10 a characteristic of the righteous is that no injustice is found among them. 'The righteous'[89] are the oppressed (96.8), the impoverished and exploited,[90] the humiliated and those who have been brought low (96.5). In not joining in, in rejecting outright the practices of the powerful, in fearlessly establishing and maintaining an alternative public, these poor and lowly show their righteousness, and the humiliated are at the same time humble.

The Jews – a people 'born for slavery', as Tacitus and the whole ancient world say of them; 'the chosen people among the nations', as they themselves say and believe – the Jews performed the miracle of the inversion of valuations, by means of which life on earth obtained a new and dangerous charm for a couple of millennia. Their prophets fused into one the expressions 'rich', 'godless', 'wicked', 'violent', 'sensual' and for the first time coined the word 'world' as a term of reproach. In this inversion of valuations (in which is also included the use of the word 'poor' as synonymous with 'saint and friend'), the significance of the Jewish people is to be found; it is with them that the slave-insurrection in morals commences (Friedrich Nietzsche, *Beyond Good and Evil*, Collected Works Vol.12, London 1909, 195, p.117).

3. 'Even if you are rich, walk humbly.' 'Humility' as the modesty of the better-off

In the previous section it had become clear that the concepts belonging within the sphere of 'humility' which served as a social designation of the lower classes could also take on an ethical dimension. But in that case the original social context always became clear. Now we must discuss passages in which this conviction has become detached. 'Humility' is understood as a positive ethical concept, but its social context is no longer with those at the bottom.

(*a*) In the book of Proverbs it appears in some passages within general rules of life.[91] Thus 15.33: 'The fear of Yahweh is instruction in wisdom, and humility ('*a̅nāwā*) goes before honour.'[92] The second clause appears word for word in 18.12: 'Before destruction a man's heart is haughty, but humility goes before honour.' In terms of content, humility is here defined by the parallelism as fear of God and in contrast to arrogance;

it may therefore be described as modesty before God and man.[93] What is meant is 'honour'. It is obvious that those envisaged here are no longer the impoverished and humiliated, but the well-to do citizens and their social reputation. That is made particularly clear by 22.4, where humility and fear of God stand side by side[94] and riches and life as well as honour are given as their reward. 29.23 is also concerned with honour. It is the modest who are not proud and arrogant who will receive honour: 'A man's pride will bring him low, but he who is lowly in spirit ($\check{s}^e pal$-$r\bar{u}a\d{h}$/ταπεινόφρονες) will obtain honour.' The speakers here do not belong with the poor; and they certainly do not belong with the wicked rich either, from whom they dissociate themselves. The understanding of the concept of humility, the distinction from the poor and the dissociation from the evildoers emerges very well in 16.19: 'It is better to be of a lowly spirit ($r\bar{u}a\d{h}$-$\check{s}^e kal$/πραΰθυμος) with the lowly ($^a n\bar{a}w\bar{i}m$/ταπείνωσις) than to divide the spoil with the proud.' But if the concept of humility which is understood in positive terms in the tradition is taken up and thus detached from its social content and generalized, it loses its focus as an attack on the prevailing (dis-)order and becomes the virtue of respectable modesty.

(*b*) That emerges even more clearly in the book of Jesus Sirach.[95] Here, too, the fact that the better-off in society are envisaged gives the concept of humility its special accent; it is even explicitly associated directly with the rich.

At one point we can see a certain parallelism of structure with remarks made by Plutarch: 'Accept whatever is brought upon you, and if fortune brings you humiliation ('$\bar{o}n\bar{i}$/ταπείνωσις), be patient. For gold is tested in the fire, and aceptable men in the furnace of humiliation ('$\bar{o}n\bar{i}$/ταπείνωσις)' (2.4f.). This is not addressed to the poor but to the rich, whose situation has become worse through fortune. Even then, it is important not to give up one's previous disposition but to continue to trust in God.

From his tradition the author knows that God exalts the lowly and humbles the exalted. But what in the tradition was hope for the poor here becomes a rule of wisdom for the rich: 'Do not ridicule a man who is bitter in soul, for there is One who abases and exalts' (7.11). The one who is now lowly could rise; and how will he stand then over against those who looked down at him and despised him?[96]

The shift in the understanding of the concept of humility becomes particularly clear in 3.17-20. If we considered the statements in vv.19f. in isolation, we would have to understand them in traditional terms in the light of the weaker members of society who set their hope on God:

'For great is the might of God, and to the lowly/humiliated (*'anāwīm/*
ταπεινοί) he reveals his counsel. For great is the might of the Lord; he
is glorified by the humble.' However, such an understanding is already
made improbable by the overall context of the book which has already
been indicated and is ruled out by the context which immediately
precedes it. For in vv.17f. the rich man is explicitly addressed: 'My son,
even if you are rich, walk in humility (*'anāwā/*πραΰτης),[97] and you will
be loved more than one who gives presents. Think yourself less than all
the great things of the world, and before God you will find mercy.'
Therefore humility as a virtue of the rich denotes a modest attitude.[98]
So vv.19f. do not have in mind those who have been humiliated and
brought low, but those rich people who do not unscrupulously exploit
their possibilities of power but rather restrain them modestly.

Whereas in the tradition the terms 'humble' and 'evildoer' are related
as opposite classes, now – detached from this social context and
understood only in ethical terms – they can be used from the perspective
of the rich to distinguish between different kinds of poor: 'Give to the
good man, but do not help the sinner; feed the humble (*māk/*ταπεινός)
but do not give to the evildoer (*zēr/*ἀσεβής)' (12.7).

The degree to which the accents are different in the book of Jesus
Sirach also emerges above all where humility is attributed to the rich
man specifically in the contrast between him and the weaker members
of sociey. In 4.8 we read: 'Incline your ear to the needy (*'anī/*πτωχός)
and return his greeting with humility/modesty (*'anāwā/*πραΰτης).' Here
humility becomes condescending friendliness, gentleness shown from
above. It is connected with the conduct of the rich towards the poor;
the structure of the relationship between them remains untouched. The
whole section 4.1-10 gives the well-to-do instructions for dealing with
the weaker member of society. He is not to hurt his sensibilities, but to
support him with gifts and stand by him when he is pressed hard in the
courts. Here the perspective is certainly that from above, but it takes
in the wretchedness of the other party, which is to be assuaged.
However, that such action is also aimed at preserving the rich man's
own status and thus the system is indicated in vv.5f.: 'Do not give the
poor any possibility of cursing you. For if in bitterness of soul he calls
down a curse upon you, his creator will hear his prayer.' The curse is
often the last resort of the oppressed against his oppressor. Not to take
the shirt off the back of the needy, but on the contrary to relieve his
position, is therefore commended to those who fear the consequences
of his curse.[99] To exaggerate somewhat: what is discussed in the first
two sections of this part, and what was promised as a hope to the

humiliated, namely a radical change in social conditions, is here to be warded off by the humility of the well-to-do, their modesty and gentleness.

The rich who are addressed in the texts of Jesus Sirach that we have just discussed are not, of course, counted among the evildoers, the haughty and the men of violence. The author's slogan is rather: 'Riches are good if they are free from sin' (13.24). The only question is whether, with his orientation on the integrated individual, he does not overlook injustice which is determined by structures. Certainly he says: 'What fellowship has a wolf with a lamb? No more has a sinner with a godly man. What peace is there between a hyena and a dog? And what peace between a rich man and a poor man? Wild asses in the wilderness are the prey of lions; likewise the poor are pastures for the rich' (13.17-19).[100] Therefore modesty and gentleness are not exactly the style of a rich man: 'Humility (*ᵃnāwā*/ταπεινότης) is an abomination to a proud man; likewise a poor man is an abomination to a rich one' (13.20). The comparison of the juxtaposition of rich and poor with natural phenomena indicates that the circumstances which the poor see as harsh must also be seen as 'natural' and thus as unchangeable. Humility understood as modesty and gentleness is then the praxis of the rich in favour of the poor which is still possible in this structure.

4. '...each should instruct his neighbour in... humility.' The understanding of the tradition of humility in Qumran

A varied use of the term 'humility', albeit within a single perspective, can be seen in the Qumran texts.[101] First of all we should note that they take up the tradition depicted in both the first two sections of this part. So in 1QH V 20-22, at the beginning of a psalm, we find: 'Praised be thou, Lord! For thou hast not forsaken the orphan and hast not despised the lowly (*rāš*)... And thou art with the humble/humiliated (*ᵃnāwīm*) when their footsteps sink, with those who fear righteousness, to lead up from the tumult all the poor of grace (*'ebyōnīm ḥesed*).' The juxtaposition of the orphan and the lowly points towards the social sphere; and the more detailed description of the humiliated/humble also makes it clear that they are in a difficult (material) situation.[102] At the same time, however, they are those 'who fear righteousness'. So the concluding designation 'all the poor of grace' will embrace both aspects, the social and the ethical. Those envisaged are the poor who are under the protection of the grace of God and who for their part trust utterly in this grace. The following text, however, is focussed on an individual, the 'teacher of righteousness', the founder of the Qumran community.[103] The context is then to be envisaged as being that he rediscovers his own experience in this tradition, that he experiences himself as the poor and the humble one who is supported by God. That is even clearer in the preceding psalm. Here too the one who prays is 'the teacher of righteousness' who designates himself not only as servant of God (v.15), but also as 'needy (*'ānī*, 13), as 'needy and lowly' (*'ānī wārāš*) and as 'poor' (*'ebyōn*, 16,18). God has delivered him from severe tribulation 'in the place of the lions' (13) 'to keep their teeth closed round about', so that they do not rend him (14). He understands his experience of suffering as a purification by God (16).[104] In the background here are the events which led to the origin of the Qumran community: the expulsion from the temple in Jerusalem by the high priest Jonathan of the 'teacher of righteousness', a priest in a high position (153-143 BC), and the withdrawal of this teacher with his followers into the wilderness.[105] 'The evildoers' of the tradition are therefore identified with the evil priest Jonathan and his entourage.[106] In 1QpHabXII there are three mentions of the evil priest, who has done evil to the 'poor' (*'ebyōnīm*) (2f.), planned their destruction (6) and plundered their possessions (9f).[107] And in 1QH II 35f. the 'teacher of righteousness' acknowledges: 'Thou hast saved my life from the hand of the powerful and wilt not let me be disheartened by their taunts, to abandon service of thee for fear of the terror of the evildoers.'

The experience of being expelled from Jerusalem, which also meant impoverishment in very specific terms, and the experience of the consolidation of the community in the wilderness despite continued hostility, form the presupposition for the acceptance of the tradition of poverty and humility. So this community can understand the sayings in Ps.37 as being applied directly to itself.[108] What is said there about the humiliated/humble (*'anāwīm*) and the righteous (*ṣaddīq*) therefore refers to them as 'the community of the poor' (*'adat hā'ebyōnīm*, II 8f.; III 9f.). Thus the designation of a social stratum becomes the designation of a group.

At two points this group takes up the concept of humility in a very distinctive way. In 1QS IX 22f. there is mention in a comparison of a slave who has to hand over his person and the work of his hands to his master as a possession and show 'humility' (*'anāwā*) towards him. This is very much in line with Greek tradition; the slave must prostrate himself because of his position and therefore also has a servile attitude – humility is seen as the servility of the lowly towards the exalted. This characterization of the slave which is made from 'above' is here taken up from 'below' as a positive example and is offered to the members of the community as a model to be imitated in the face of those with other views on whom they are dependent, in order to conceal and sustain their hatred against them:[109] 'eternal hatred against the men of the pit in the spirit of concealment' (21f.). We are probably to understand a command in 1QS XI 1f. in the same way; 'to answer the arrogant in humility ('*anāwā*) and with a contrite spirit the oppressors who point with the finger, speak lies and obtain riches.'

There is a completely new aspect in the understanding of humility when it does not describe a relationship between the lowly and the better-off, whether as subservience on the one side and modesty and gentleness on the other, but is to issue in mutuality. The framework here is provided by the monastic-type community. 1QS V 1-7, which binds the members to the community and condemns individualistic deviations, adds to humility and a humble life-style, in a series, faithfulness, righteousness, justice and steadfast love. Here humility may especially mean voluntarily taking one's place in the group by suppressing individual interests, in other words, loyalty to the community. The continuation of the text in vv.24f. is the admonition that 'each should instruct his neighbour in truthfulness, humility and steadfast love'. In this context, for which mutuality, if not equality,[110] is a decisive factor, humility makes the admonotion a truly brotherly one and prevents it from being given 'from above'.

IV

'...and exalts the humble.'
God's option for 'humility' in the primitive Christian tradition

Primitive Christianity generally is influenced not only by the Old Testament-Jewish tradition but also by the Greek-Hellenistic world, and both spheres had already come together before Christianity in Hellenistic Judaism. That is also paticularly true of talk of 'humility'. I shall now indicate some stages in the understanding of this concept and its development in Christianity. Here it will emerge, first, that what makes the term 'humility' so suspect today – its prime associations with subservience and servile obedience – can already be seen at the end of the first century; secondly, however, it emerges that the primitive Christian tradition was essentially moulded by that of the Old Testament and Judaism, which have been discussed in the previous two sections of this book.

1. ' Come to me, slaves...' God's solidarity with the humiliated

(a) There is a pointed reassessment of the Old Testament-Jewish tradition in Matt.11.28-30.[1] It has a clearly recognizable structure. I shall indicate this by the most literal translation possible, printed line for line, which I shall then describe in order to obtain a starting point for further questions.

1 Come to me, all who toil and are burdened
2 And I will give you rest.
3 Take my yoke upon you and learn from me.
4 For I am gentle and lowly of heart.
5 And you will find rest for your souls.
6 My yoke is easy and my burden light.

Two imperatives form the basic structure (1.3). The first invites a particular group of people to come to the speaker; the second defines the first more precisely with the admonition of this speaker to take on his yoke and to learn from him. A promise is attached to each imperative (2.5): the first is direct; a reason is given before the second. Both promises are identical in content. According to the first, the speaker wants to give what he promises to those who are addressed; according to the second they wil find it when they heed his admonition. The second imperative is followed by two reasons, separated by the second promise (4.6); they correspond in content. The first characterizes the nature of the speaker, the second the nature of his yoke. With the word 'yoke' the second reason (6) provides a reference back to the second imperative (3), and beyond that to the first imperative, as the idea of the yoke is also associated with the 'burdened' who are mentioned there. The mention of the 'burdened' also provides a reference to the burden of the speaker mentioned at the end of the last line. We can also see a conscious structure in the change of subject between individual lines. The second person plural in the first, third and fifth lines is followed in the second and fourth lines by the first person singular and in the last line by the third person singular with the possessive pronouns in the first person singular. Thus Matt.11.28-30 turns out to be a carefully composed passage in which a speaker described by the reasons he gives admonishes a particular group of people and gives them a promise. This raises further questions: who are the people addressed here? What are the qualifications of the speaker? What is he inviting people to? What is he promising? So we must also ask whether it is possible to identify who is speaking.

Those who are addressed are first described as 'the toilers' (οἱ κοπιῶντες). The most immediate and obvious usage of the Greek word is to denote those people who have to work hard, who toil and sweat their guts out, who are exhausted by strenuous work which wears them out. According to Adolf Schlatter 'the idea of .. performing work depends on κοπιᾶν with the subsidiary notion that work is strenuous and wearisome, so that exerting one's strength leads to exhaustion.'[2] Certainly this word can also be used in a metaphorical sense, but that would have to be indicated in some way, which is not the case here. Thus if there are no objections as a result of the following comments an attempt must be made to understand the text in the usual sense of this word, which means hard labour, manual labour.[3] So in social terms it envisages people from the lowest class.

The same goes for the second term describing the people who are addressed here, which does not allow any kind of addition in another direction. The 'burdened' (οἱ πεφορτισμένοι) are those who have to carry heavy loads. It is therefore quite appropriate for an exegete to speak here of those who are 'exhausted and humbled'[4] and for Walter Jens to translate the first line of the paragraph like this: 'Hey! Come to me, slaves, under the yoke and worn out with your burdens.'[5] The mention of the burdened also introduces the idea of the yoke, since they carry their burdens with the help of a yoke. Moreover the yoke also contains the idea of the rule that is exercised,[6] whether in the directly economic sphere by the one who controls the labourers, or in the wider political sphere. This connection is made explicitly in the lament of the oppressed from the epistle of Enoch which I quoted in the previous section.[7]

Luise Schottroff understands Matt.11.28-30 in the light of the latter: the people suffer under the violent use of power.[8] 'In Jesus' call the situation of the people is described as distress caused by the rule of violence which puts people in a position comparable to the exertions of hard physical work.'[9] She is certainly right in pointing out that the political dimension may not be excluded. But what justification is there in regarding the 'hard physical work' of which the text speaks merely as a point of comparison? The exercise of rule – whether in Roman provincial administration or by local vassals ruling by favour of Rome – was manifested not least by all kinds of demands for intensified work. So it may be appropriate to keep to the original meaning of hard and servile work for 'those who toil and are burdened'.

However, the usual interpretation of Matt.11.28-30 goes in a quite different direction. It understands burden and yoke as the burden and yoke of the law.[10] For this, reference is made within the New Testament to Matt.23.4; Acts 15.10, 28f.[11] In Matt.23.4 it is said of 'the Pharisees and scribes' in respect of the legal regulations which they make: 'They bind heavy burdens, hard to bear, and lay them on men's shoulders; but they themselves will not move them with their finger.' According to Acts 15.10 Peter speaks of the law of Moses (v.5) as a yoke which must not be put on the necks of the disciples, 'which neither our fathers nor we have been able to bear'; and therefore according to 15.28f. the Gentile Christians must observe only certain minimum prescriptions, and otherwise 'no greater burden' is to be imposed on them. Furthermore, Jewish texts are cited which speak of the yoke of the law or of wisdom identified with the law. One need only mention the song of praise to wisdom in Sirach 51.13-30. In v.25 we read : 'Buy wisdom without money! Bow your necks under her yoke and bear her burden!'[12] However, Schottroff is to be followed in noting over against the assumption based on these texts that the law is also in view in Matt.11.28-30, that wherever mention of yoke and burden denotes the law or legal prescriptions, that is also said explicitly or follows clearly from the context, which is not the case here.[13] There is no indication of such an understanding, at least for the pre-Matthaean tradition.[14]

So the first point to be noted is that the terms used for the people who are addressed denotes dependent workers who have to wear themselves out earning their meagre daily wage.[15]

The speaker who addresses them says that he is one of them, in that he describes himself as being 'meek and lowly of heart'. This translation is probably not precise enough if one notes the tradition which is taken up here. The juxtaposition of the two terms (πραΰς and ταπεινός) makes it evident that the former cannot be understood along the lines of the Graeco-Roman tradition, where πραΰς/*clementia* denotes the virtue of the ruler.[16] It is not a matter of replacing a harsh rule with a humane one.[17] πραΰς and ταπεινός stand side by side in the Septuagint as a translation of '*ānī wādāl*.[18] This is a designation for the impoverished and humiliated who deliberately accept their situation, set their hope on God, withdraw from the complex of violence and practise a different form of justice and righteousness from those who rule by force.[19] This connection is deliberately affirmed by the addition of the words 'of heart' to 'lowly'.[20]

The speaker invites those whom he addresses to come to him, to take his yoke upon them and learn of him. The original context of this call seems most likely to have been discipleship of Jesus. Here Jesus calls people out of oppressed and oppressive circumstances to his discipleship, the new community of his disciples which escapes the conditions of exploitation and domination and in which these conditions are no longer to hold.[21] In contrast to the words of the oppressed in the epistle of Enoch who have to say, 'We found no place to flee to and escape from them,'[22] here Jesus can offer such a place with his discipleship. It may seem surprising that those who are in any case already under the yoke, those who bear the yoke, but who are called out of their situation, must again take a yoke upon them.[23] The statement here is evidently in the perspective of those who cannot imagine any other life than being under the yoke. So is this yet another form of exercising lordship? However, the particular feature of this invitation of Jesus is that the one who calls men under his yoke, the one who is himself lowly and humble in that he takes the cause of those brought low and humiliated, is in solidarity with them. To learn from him can only mean to learn solidarity. Talk of the yoke indeed uses the language of lordship, but the lordship is in fact transcended.[24] So the yoke can also be described paradoxically as 'not oppressive'[25] and the burden as light. It is not the case that there is now no more to do and to bear, but the burdens are tolerable in solidarity with one another because each individual is supported by the community of brothers and sisters.

So Jesus can promise refreshment to those who are worn out to the point of exhaustion. 'I will give you rest.' 'You will find rest for yourselves[26].' That is the promise of the call to discipleship. It is of elementary simplicity and corresponds antithetically with the direct weight of the burden. Those who constantly have to work to the point of exhaustion have the most pressing desire to be able to rest.[27] 'Liberation from physical and spiritual afflictions, troubles and burdens of all kinds is part of the eschatological message of Jesus and is the direct theme of his work. Hence the call' not only 'embraces those who sigh under such loads'[28] but here and now is addressed only to them.

The second promise is a quotation from Jer. 6.16.[29] In that context it is an attack on false assertions of peace, where greed, deception and exploitation prevail. Peace is only to be found where the word and instruction of God are noted, where violence ceases and the oppressed obtain their rights. In Jer.6.16 the promise of rest appears in an oracle of God. It is for those who 'ask for the ancient paths, where the good way is and walk in it', who demonstrate 'the loyalty of the people towards Yahweh'.[30] In Matt.11.28-30 Jesus promises rest to those who come to him and learn from him. His disciples will tread 'the way of salvation' (Jer.6.16). This is a lofty claim. In formal terms Jesus' words are like those of wisdom in Prov.8. She attracts and admonishes in v.4: 'To you, O men, I call, and my cry is to the sons of men. O simple ones, learn prudence, O foolish men, pay attention.'[31] It is clear that the teaching and call here is 'from above'. In accordance with that the promise consists in 'riches and honour' (vv.18, 21). Jesus does not promise riches to the poor, but the kingdom of God, in which the hungry will be full and those who weep will laugh (Luke 6.20f.). Accordingly he promises those who are exhausted that they can rest. The aim here is not a land of milk and honey, but what must happen. For this, 'humility' is needed. Jesus' humility is shown in the way in which he enters into solidarity with the humiliated and those who have been brought low.

If the saying that is handed down twice each in the Gospels of Matthew and Luke, that the one who humbles himself will be exalted and the one who exalts himself will be brought low (Matt.18.4; 23.12; Luke 14.11; 18.4),[32] derives from Jesus himself it could take on a particular profile in the context I have just demonstrated. Self-abasement in the way in which a person enters into solidarity with the lowly and the humiliated has as its fruits exaltation, namely the enrichment of life in a new community. Hence the humiliation mentioned as the consequence of self-exaltation is to be defined as the impoverishment of a life which is in isolation. The passive in the main clauses, the logical subject of which must be taken to be God, expresses the fact that God is behind this combination of humiliation and exaltation.

The reference of this logion to the fellowship of Jesus' disciples and thus to the community follows from its inclusion in the Gospel of Matthew. In the scene in 18.1-5, which Matthew has created, the disciples ask who is to be the greatest in the kingdom of heaven. Jesus puts a child in their midst and asks them to become like children. 'Whoever humbles himself like this child, he is the greatest in the kingdom of heaven' (v.4).[33] Greatness demonstrates itself specifically in a renunciation of being great and of wanting to tower over others. Matthew pursues an anti-hierarchical tendency and puts forward a model based on brothers and sisters. The second passage makes that even clearer. In 23.8-12 Matthew presupposes that there are scribes and teachers in the community, but he forbids them to be called 'rabbi', 'father' and 'master'. All in the community have Christ as their teacher and master and God as their father. That makes them brothers and sisters to one another (v.8b). This relationship is made specific in service for the community: 'The greatest among you shall be your servant' (v.11). The fact that the saying about humiliation and exaltation in v.12 brings this passage to an end makes it clear that it refers to fellowship within the community.

Its place in the Gospel of Luke is quite different: here the individual is the focal point. In 14.11 it stands as the essence of the rule of wisdom not to take the best seat at a wedding feast in case one is asked to move by the host and thus shamed before the eyes of all, but rather to take the lowest place, so that the host asks one to go up higher, thus singling one out before the company (14.7-10).[34] In 18.14b Luke ends the parable of the Pharisee and the publican with this saying. That makes it a paradigm for the behaviour of the individual, an indication of how he can gain recognition before God.

'*Luke 18.14 improved.* He that humbleth himself wishes to be exalted' (Friedrich Nietzsche, *Human, All too Human*, I 87, Collected Works 6, London 1909, 88).

' "Whoever exalts himself will be humbled and whoever humbles himself..." But if one knows that, can count on it and does count on it, one humbles oneself by exalting oneself and is therefore exalted. And the important thing is to know to what link in the the chain to count in order really to be exalted or humiliated.

This biblical saying, though it is not one of the most interesting, thus gives rise to a sport to which many people have succumbed and from which some cunning spirits think that they can profit very well. Lichtenberg notes: "I find a doer of small things far more honest than a doer of big things..."

It is better in any case to judge people by their positive side than by their other properties, not according to whether they abase or exalt themselves. It is better to leave this completely out of consideration' (Ludwig Hohl, *Die Notizen oder Von der unvoreiligen Versöhnung* VII, 94, Frankfurt am Main 1984, 409).

(*b*) Mary's Magnificat, which Luke has taken over (Luke 1.46-55),[35] is very much in line with Old Testament-Jewish tradition. It should be seen as a protest song. The speaker begins by praising God as saviour, 'since he has looked on the humiliation/lowliness (ταπείνωσις) of his handmaid/slave (δούλη)' (v.48). The description of Mary as a maid or slave points to the social sphere. Certainly the term 'handmaid of God' can be understood in a transferred sense,[36] but the second part (vv.53-55),[37] which draws sweeping conclusions from the first, makes it quite clear that the one who utters the Magnificat cannot be a person of high standing. The birth of the messiah Jesus from the lowly maiden, who as a result has been exalted, already includes the eschatological elevation of the humbled and the fall from power of the rich man:[38] God 'shows strength with his arm, and scatters the proud in the imagination of their hearts. He casts down the mighty from their thrones and exalts the humiliated. He fills the hungry with good things and the rich he sends empty away' (vv.51-53). The positive and negative sequences produced at this point are clear. On the one hand are the arrogant, the powerful and the rich,[39] whom God scatters, casts down from their thrones and sends empty away, and on the other there are the lowly/humiliated (ταπεινοί) and hungry whom he hears and to whom he gives good things in abundance. With this positive action God accepts Israel and fulfils the promise given to the fathers (vv.54f.). The humbled and humiliated who adopt this protest song as their own and join in it feel themselves to be those whose backs God strengthens, so that they can now already walk upright.

(*c*) The last work we need to discuss in this section is the letter of James. There is a clear contrast between the poor and the rich, the exaltation of the one and the humiliation of the other, in 1.9-11: 'Let the lowly (ταπεινός) brother boast in his exaltation, and the rich in his humiliation (ταπείνωσις), because like the flower of the grass he will pass away. For the sun rises with its scorching heat and withers the grass, its flower falls and its beauty perishes. So will the rich man fade away in the midst of his pursuits.' The contrast with the rich shows the 'humiliated brother' to be the Christian who is characterized by poverty and the humiliations associated with it.[40] As there is mention on the one hand of the 'humiliated brother' the reference on the other hand could be to 'the rich (brother)',[41] and not to 'the rich' generally. But that is very improbable. In the first place the text explicitly and definitively forecasts a negative end for the rich;[42] and secondly, at other places in which he speaks of the rich James is clearly referring only to non-Christians.[43] He certainly also knows well-to-do Christians,[44] but he does not speak of them as rich. Both the humiliated brother and the rich man are to boast. 'That of which a person may boast is that which is held as a sure and eternal possession.'[45] The humiliated poor man has nothing in his hand; but he does have the promise of God who exalts the lowly. This tradition is taken up here. As is shown by the future forms on the other side, in the case of the rich the thought here is of the eschatological action of God which will change the world by helping the poor, humbled and abased, to gain their rights. The substance of the boast of the poor is not that they are 'rich in faith' (2.5) and as a result are 'already raised to a "height" by God'.[46] The humiliated brother does not boast of his rich faith but only of that of which he is certain: God's promise.

On the other hand, what the rich person who has so much can be equally sure of is what God will prepare for him: his humiliation. This is clearly portrayed in the picture of the withering of the grass, and indeed there is the explicit statement that he will pass away and vanish – with no ifs and buts. Thus the boast of the rich man amounts to nothing; and so the invitation to him to boast is simply bitter irony.[47]

The invitation, understood in this way, is precisely matched by 5.1: 'Come now, you rich, weep and howl for the miseries that are coming over you.' The fate of the rich announced here, for which they should already howl, is the present experience of the poor whose wretched situation makes them howl. The following text makes it clear that the announcement of the judgment has its basis in the conduct of the rich or, to put it more sharply, in riches themselves and the way in which they have been gained. They rest on ruthless exploitation: 'Behold, the wages of the labourers who mowed your fields, which you kept back by fraud, cry out' (v.4).[48] This exploitation is disguised by a class justice which is not afraid of murder: 'You have condemned, you have killed the innocent man' (v.6).[49] Of riches gained in this way James says: 'Your riches have rotted and your garments are moth-eaten. Your gold and silver have rusted, and their rust will be evidence against you' (vv.2f.).[50] The 'gathering of treasures' (v.3) produces a useless superfluity on the one hand and misery on the other. The principle of maximizing gain has become an unjust system which finally also expresses itself in the life of luxury led by the rich: 'You have lived on the earth in luxury and in pleasure; you have fattened your hearts in a day of slaughter' (v.5).[51] With this comment James makes it clear that God is on the side of the poor who suffer injustice and will bring about change.

The community, too, is oppressed by the rich: 'Is it not the rich who oppress you, is it not they who drag you into court? Is it not they who blaspheme that honourable name by which you are called?' (2.6f.).[52] Nevertheless, they are in danger of imitating the rich. The behaviour of the rulers becomes the prevalent model of conduct and thus also determines the conduct of those who are oppressed by them. That is clear not only from the instance presented in 2.2-4, when a well dressed and a badly dressed non-Christian come into the assembly and one is taken heed of but not the other.[53] It also becomes clear in the remarks in 4.1-3. James notes that there are fights and disputes in the community; there is that 'jealous disposition which would like most of all to liquidate its opponent';[54] there is covetousness and the desire for extravagance. To allow oneself to be shaped in this way by the prevailing model of behaviour is love of worldliness which amounts to adultery towards God and hostility to him (v.4), and this makes him jealous (v.5). In this connection James cites Prov.3.34: 'God opposes the proud, but gives grace to the humble (ταπεινοί)' (v.6). If that is the case, the community must renounce the behaviour described earlier, since this is the behaviour of the arrogant. This leads to the admonitions in vv.7-10. Here v.9 is particularly striking because it contains a similar invitation to that addressed to the rich in 5.1: 'Be wretched and mourn and weep. Let your laughter be turned to mourning and your joy to dejection.' The community is not to join in the laughter and the self-satisfied complacency of the rich, is not to share in their world. The invitation to be wretched, mourn and weep is here given to those who behave in the way the world behaves, namely the world of the rich and powerful. Instead of imitating them it is important to show solidarity with those whose situation is dominated by wretchness, lamentation and tears. This leads James to invite them to 'humble yourselves (ταπεινώθητε) before the Lord'; to those showing such humiliation, following his tradition James gives the promise 'and he will exalt you' (v.10). Here he is thinking within the framework of the community. He is concerned with its unity, which helps towards such humility.[55] As 2.15f. makes clear, part of this is that community members who lack clothing and food have their needs satisfied by the community.[56]

2. 'In humility count others better than yourselves.' 'Humility' as
the condition for a new community

In this section I shall be discussing passages from the letters of Paul and
writings in the Pauline tradition. An investigation of the understanding
of the concept of humility in Paul is interesting in several ways. First,
one can see the influence of various traditions, Greek and Jewish, in
the assessment of Paul's activity by others and by himself. These
traditions also emerge characteristically in the apostle's own evaluation
of the social situation which can be described in various ways. Finally,
we can see from the christological foundation for the call for humility
in his communities where his talk of 'humility' ultimately leads and what
gives it its particular stamp.

(*a*) In II Cor.10.1 Paul speaks of himself as one 'who (is) humble
(ταπεινός) when face to face with you but bold to you when I am away'.
That here he is taking up a charge made against him emerges clearly
from v.10, where he quotes as a saying circulated about him: 'his letters
are weighty and strong, but his bodily presence is weak, and his speech
of no account'. In this context ταπεινός in v.1 is recognizably stamped
by the Greek tradition. It characterizes Paul's appearance as lowly,
grovelling, servile, weak.[57] The specific occasion for this assessment
may lie in Paul's failure on his so-called intermediate visit to Corinth to
put to rights the community, which had split into factions and had
largely turned against him: he had to travel on to Ephesus without
having achieved success.[58] On this visit Paul had had a particularly
humiliating experience: he says that wrong was done him and that he
was troubled.[59]

Paul does not simply counter the taunt that his personal appearance
is lowly by saying that the taunt is wrong. He explains in II Cor.12.7-11
that he does not want to be strong, but deliberately accepts his weakness;
we shall not go further into that here. He also accepts the humiliation he
has suffered, not as a human judgment, but from God. But significantly,
here he puts the stress elsewhere. In II Cor.12.20f. he writes: 'For I fear
that perhaps I may come and find you not what I wish, and that you
may find me not what you wish; that perhaps there may be quarrelling,
jealousy, anger, selfishness, slander, gossip, conceit and disorder. I fear
that when I come again my God may humble (ταπεινώσῃ) me before
you, and I may have to mourn over many of those who sinned before
and have not repented of 'the impurity, immorality and licentiousness
which they have practised'. What Paul had to suffer on the intermediate
visit on which he looks back here, he experienced as abasement and

humiliation. But at this point he mentions God as subject. From God he accepts for himself the humiliation that he has suffered, but without approving of the event which brought it about. The comment about his weakness is a matter of principle, but not that about his humiliation. He does not want to have such an experience again. The judgment that Paul is 'lowly' in his personal appearance is certainly based above all on the fact that he had to leave Corinth without achieving success. Acceptance of the humiliation imposed on him certainly cannot mean abandoning the community. He continues to fight for it, and when he hears that it has been restored by Titus he sees this as the exaltation by God of those who have been humiliated. So he interprets this experience with the help of Old Testament tradition when in II Cor.7.6 he writes: 'God who comforts the downcast comforted us by the coming of Titus', who reported to him that the Corinthian community had been won back.[60] However, it might be not least this knowledge that God comforts the downcast which makes Paul accept the humiliations, not in order to be resigned to them, but to fight them.

(*b*) While Paul is hardly looking for actual humiliations, the decision to lead his life in lowly circumstances, to live as a 'lowly' one, is a matter of principle for him. That is indicated by Phil.4.10-20, in which he expresses his gratitude for support from the community of Philippi. While he stresses his joy about this, at the same time he points out that he is not speaking out of need. There is no doubt that he is in need, but he does not attach any importance to this, nor is he concerned to be relieved of this need, as he has learned to be content in his situation (v.11). He then continues: 'I know both how to live in humble circumstances (ταπεινοῦσθαι) and to live in abundance; in any and all circumstances I have learned the secret of being full and enduring hunger, living in plenty and suffering want' (v.12). ταπεινοῦσθαι is parallel to 'hunger' and 'suffer want' and opposed to 'live in plenty' and 'be full' and is thus clearly determined by the material situation. Therefore here it does not denote a voluntary renunciation of being filled, and does not therefore have the technical meaing of 'fast',[61] but describes the situation of need among the poor, who do not have enough to eat.[62] Paul joyfully gives thanks for the help which has come to him in such a situation, but also points out that this help was not absolutely necessary – and that includes the consequence that as far as he was concerned it need not have been given. In doing this he points to a basic significance of his way of life as one of the 'lowly'. Anyone who says that he can live either way, in need or in abundance,[63] was hardly a poor man to begin with. Therefore for Paul his life-style as one of the 'lowly' is not a compulsion laid on him from the beginning, but a deliberate choice. That is made even clearer by the passage that we must go on to discuss.

In II Cor.11.7 Paul asks: 'Did I commit a sin in abasing myself (ἐμαυτὸν ταπεινῶν) so that you might be exalted, because I preached God's gospel without cost to you?' What he has in mind here is that he was involved in manual labour to provide the material basis for his missionary activity. He describes that as humbling himself. So here we find the same negative evaluation of manual labour as in the Greek and Latin literature that has come down to us.[64] Paul's attitude might also presuppose the same social basis, i.e. an exalted social status: clearly he was not a manual worker to begin with.[65] However, the decisive point is that while Paul shares the negative evaluation of manual work common among the better-off in the Graeco-Roman world,[66] he engages in this work, of which he has a negative estimation, of his own free will and quite certainly does not see his action in a completely negative way. In this self-abasement he is extremely 'un-Greek' and 'un-Roman'. He shows solidarity with those whom God has chosen, the insignificant and the despised (I Cor.1.27f.), and is not a burden to them (II Cor.11.9), so that they are exalted. Though he originally had the perspective of someone in a high position he adopts the perspective of the insignificant by his life-style. That is the way in which he shows his humility.

(c) Paul does not invite the better-off Christians in his community to imitate his way of living. It is part of his particular apostolic existence.[67] But the attitude which is evident here and the practice of solidarity with the insignificant, this 'humility', is also the object and aim of his paraenesis. So he writes in Rom.12.16, within a series of admonitions: 'Do not be haughty, but associate with the lowly (τοῖς ταπεινοῖς).'[68] Immediately after that he asks people not to be wise on their own account. That would be a wisdom gained apart from the others and with personal interests in mind, orientated 'above'. It goes with looking for promotion, the quest for upward mobility. Such wisdom and such a concern disrupt solidarity and lead to competition.[69] However, Paul is aiming at 'harmony with one another', which he calls for at the beginning of v.16. It can come about in the community only if the community is orientated on the possibilities, the needs and the distress of its weakest members – if it allows itself to 'descend' with them, is in solidarity with them.[70] The content of the admonition of v.13a accords with this: 'Contribute to the needs of the saints!'[71]

Karl Barth, *The Epistle to the Romans*, London 1933, spoke of Christianity as follows in his exegesis of Rom.12.16: 'It hears the joists creaking mysteriously. Christianity cannot simply disregard what it has seen and heard. We can now understand why Christianity loves the poor and the oppressed, the sorrowful, the hungry, and the thirsty' (463). 'Christianity displays a certain inclination to side with those who are immature, sullen, and depressed, with those who come off badly and are, in consequence, ready for revolution' (ibid.). But cf. also the dialectic – unconsidered but clearly influential – extending up to 466 which relativizes 'what, in the concrete happenings of life, is at any given moment really *high* and what is really *lowly*' (464). In the first edition, never translated into English (*Der Römerbrief*, 1919, ed. Hermann Schmidt 1985), in Rom.12.16 Barth had spoken of 'one-sided and resolute partisanship'. 'You do not belong to the lords. Nor can you be neutral and do justice to all people. No matter what, you belong to the ordinary people... For while God is a God of both the Jews *and* the Gentiles he is not a God of both the exalted *and* the lowly, but one-sidedly a God of the lowly. Nor is he a God of both great *and* small, but without distinction a God of the small' (489f.).

Friedrich-Wilhelm Marquardt ('Gott oder Mammon – aber: Theologie und Ökonomie bei Martin Luther', in *Einwürfe* 1, Munich 1983 [165-216], 187-200, the quotation comes from 198) has shown that 'evangelical *humilitas*' orientates Luther's understanding of God, Christ and the gospel originally on the stratum of the poor. Here Rom.12.16 and Phil.2 are particularly important for Luther: cf. the quotations in Marquardt, 198, 199.

So it does not seem to be a coincidence that where Paul explicitly calls for humility he has in mind the fellowship of the community. That is the case in Phil.2.3. This verse comes within the complex of 2.1-11, so we must be aware of its construction if we are to understand the call for humility in the right way. In v.1 Paul begins with four conditional statements giving the presupposition on which he formulates the imperatives which follow in vv.2-4. He goes on to develop the second imperative[72] in participial phrases. He then sums up the developed imperatives in v.5a in one brief statement and in v.5b indicates their norm, which he again develops in vv.6-11 by citing the famous Christ-hymn.[73] The following line-for-line translation attempts to demonstrate the structure of the text.

So if there is any promise and claim[74] in Christ,
    if there is any incentive of love,
    if there is any participation in the Spirit,
    if there is any affection and sympathy,
        complete my joy.

Be of the same mind,
> having the same love,
> being in full accord and of one mind.
> Do nothing from selfishness or conceit,
> but in humility count others better than yourselves.
> Let each of you look not only to his own interests,
> but also to the interests of others.
> Have this mind among yourselves,
>> which you have in Christ Jesus.

The admonition follows 'in (Jesus) Christ' (vv.1,5); the indicative includes the imperative.[75] Thus the structure already makes it clear that the Christ-event is the basis and norm for the action of the community. Paul addresses the community as an ethical subject and as an object of the saving action of God. In v.1 he addresses it in terms of its Christian experience and wants it to prove itself as a Christian community. Here what he has in mind is not eternal preservation – he had discussed that in 1.27-30 – but what goes on within the community. So in many different ways he mentions unanimity as a guideline. In vv.3f. he shows how this is to be attained in both a negative and a positive way. Selfishness and self-seeking, the urge to excel in comparison with others, are ruled out... A concern to rise higher gets in the way of the harmony of the community. As a positive counterpart Paul suggests regarding the other person as being higher than oneself. That attitude is brought about by the 'humility' ($\tau\alpha\pi\epsilon\iota\nu o\phi\rho o\sigma\acute{\upsilon}\nu\eta$) which puts one's own person 'below' that of the other and is therefore exactly the opposite to the concern for self-improvement. Humility is concerned not with one's own advantage but with that of others. At this point it is important to stress once again that these admonitions are not addressed to isolated individuals but to individuals as members of the community.[76]

The trend within society goes against this. I showed in Part II how during the Roman empire society was marked strongly by a concern for upward social mobility.[77] That against such a background Paul invites not isolated individuals but members of the community to behave in the opposite way to that prevalent in society makes this sphere 'in Christ' another society, an alternative society as a society which shows solidarity. But in that case 'humility' is not individual renunciation[78] but the basic condition for a new society which really is all-inclusive.

While the sphere 'in Christ' is to be given specific form by such conduct on the part of those who inhabit it, this pre-existing sphere is itself already its basis and norm. Paul explains how far that is the case by citing the hymn in vv.6-11.

Against the background of the society of the early empire in which loyalty towards a master furthered upward social mobility, Gerd Theissen has attempted on the basis of this hymn to understand 'faith in the exalted Lord as an offer of loyalty in ascent for everyone'.[79] However, it seems to me that neither the hymn nor its Pauline context correspond to social reality, but rather run contrary to it.[80] Still,with Theissen it must be stressed that the interpretation of this text may not be seen apart from the social context to which it is addressed. He uses terms which denote social status: slave and lord. Also with the help of these terms he describes descent and ascent. Social descent and ascent within the society of those who first heard this text therefore form a natural background against which they might understand it.

If one reads the hymn against this background, its first part (vv.6-8) appears as the description of the complete opposite to a career. The one about whom no higher statement can be made, who was 'in the mode of being of God', did not hold on to this equality with God 'as prey that he had found' (v.6),[81] 'but emptied himself and adopted the mode of being of a slave' (v.7a). 'The word "servant" or "slave" offers the greatest possible contrast to God and his lordship.'[82] What we have here is 'the maximum dissonance of status'.[83] Christ 'emptied himself' from one mode of being to another; literally we read 'he made himself empty',[84] abandoned supreme power and surrendered himself to the utmost helplessness. The couplet in v.7a is to be understood in an even more pointed way: it looks at the self-surrender involved in assuming the state of a slave, in the context of the social experience of selling oneself into slavery. Such selling of oneself was a last resort, embarked on in order to survive – perhaps also in the vague hope of a later freedom. Here the self-surrender takes place from the highest position; and it has as its goal the shameful death of the cross. This underlines once again how this course is precisely the opposite of a career.

This opposite of a career is described further and brought to a head as follows. The one like God, 'being born in the likeness of man' (v.7b),[85] 'emptied himself (ἐταπείνωσεν)' (v.8a) and become 'lowly'. It is clear both from the tradition history of this concept and from the preceding context which spoke of the 'mode of existence of a slave' that here too the social sphere is being kept in mind. Subsequently the humiliation is explained in two ways: first, that he was 'subservient[86] to death' (v.8b): he remained a slave all his life, continued helpless to the end. Then this way into lowliness comes to its ultimate conclusion with the mention of the death of the cross, which in this context is to be characterized even more sharply than the shameful death of a slave.[87] In this way Christ goes his own way from self-sacrifice in lifelong helplessness to the lowest conceivable nadir, a 'point of no return'.

It should be clear that this descent, down to the depths, is not the friendly condescension of a potentate. At this point the difference between Graeco-Roman 'homage' and Old Testament-Jewish 'humility' becomes clear. Pliny reports that after the Emperor Trajan had nominated candidates to the senate, he went to each of them and kissed them, 'stepping down to our level'. 'So that with sincere admiration the entire Senate acclaimed you as the more noble and revered. For when a man can improve no more on his supreme position, the only way he can rise still higher is by stepping down, confident in his greatness. There is nothing the fortune of princes has less to fear than the risk of being brought too low (*humilitas*).'[88] By contrast the humiliation of Christ in the hymn in Phil.2 is an act of the deepest solidarity.

The way in which the drunken Herr Puntila wants to be 'common' with his servant Matti is quite different.
Puntila: Brother, we must talk about money.
Matti: Certainly.
Puntila: But it's common to talk about money.
Matti: Then don't let's talk about money.
Puntila: Wrong. Why shouldn't we be common? That's my question. Aren't we free men?
Matti: No.
Puntila: Oh, yes we are, and as free men we can do what we want, and now we want to be common... I would like to have nothing. That would please me most. Look, money stinks. My dream would be to have nothing and for us to walk through beautiful Finland, or at least go in a little two-seater that would take us anywhere with just a drop of petrol, and now and then, when we were tired, we would go into an inn like this and have one for the road. You could do that with your eyes shut, brother.
(Bertolt Brecht, *Herr Puntila und sein Knecht Matti*, Scene 1, in id., *Gesammelte Werke* IV, Frankfurt am Main 1967, 1618-20).

This hymn might have been written by people who themselves had an inferior position. These people, whose life is full of experiences of lowliness and humility, discover that Christ has joined them, and in Christ, God himself. So their situation is not hopeless.

For all power belongs to the one who has come to be in deepest solidarity with them: 'Therefore God has also highly exalted him and given him the name above all names' (v.9). The 'therefore' at the begining of this second part of the hymn draws its logic fom the Old Testament-Jewish tradition that God exalts the humiliated. The one who has here undergone the deepest humiliation experiences the highest possible exaltation. So now there is mention of an upward movement. The 'point of no return' is turned. But this upward movement is not a career in the sense of upward social mobility, nor a way upwards, which often enough leads over corpses. That is already made clear by a grammatical distinction between the first part and the second. In the first part, in the descent, the career that is not a career, Christ himself is the subject of the action; he actively takes the way down below. However, in the second part, in the upward movement, he is exclusively the object of the divine action. He himself does not follow the 'way up'; he is exalted 'so that every knee should bow, in heaven and on earth and under the earth, and every tongue confess that Jesus Christ is Lord to the glory of God the Father' (vv.10f.).[89] In this way, through his exaltation by God, through his becoming *the* Lord, Christ's Lordship not only challenges the exercise of other rule but is itself also of another nature. It is not the lordship of a man who is made god, as is the case with the Roman emperor,[90] which therefore can come about only from a lordship which appoints lower orders; it is not the rule of someone 'on the up and up', who has been hardened and distorted by the hard 'way up' and now proves to be particularly brutal to his subordinates.[91] It is the rule of one who descends, the one like God who has exposed himself to all power and shown solidarity with the least of people on his descent.[92] His rule comes about in a praxis of solidarity with those over whom he rules. Such a praxis leaves room for his 'humility'.

(*d*) The concept of humility also appears in Deutero-Pauline texts related to the fellowship in the community. Thus in Col.3.12 there is the admonition: 'Put on, then, as God's chosen ones, holy and beloved, compassion, kindness, lowliness (ταπεινοφροσύνη), meekness (πραΰτης) and patience.' Here humility appears within a series of virtues which further the common life of the community. That this is seen as a community of brothers and sisters on an equal footing is shown by the preceding v.11, which rules out ethnic, religious, social and cultural divisions for the new human being in the sphere of the community and stresses Christ as the power which permeates all things and establishes unity.[93] All the virtues enumerated here are thus connected with mutuality; one member does not have humility as lowliness, another meekness as condescending respect. The aspect of mutuality is also stressed in v.13, which follows, when it admonishes members with great solemnity to bear one another's burdens and to forgive, and in this connection refers to 'the action of the Lord which determines the basis and direction of the actions of believers'.[94] Finally, all the virtues of love are suggested as a 'bond of perfection' (v.14). It is clear from this that gentleness in v.12 cannot be understood in the light of the Graeco-Roman tradition of the virtue of the ruler, but comes from the Old Testament-Jewish tradition and is synonymous with humility. As in Phil.2.1-4, 'humility' at this point thus has the negative character of refraining from emphasizing one's own person in the fellowship of the community, forgoing competition and rivalry, and positively encouraging each to help the other.[95]

(*e*) The use of Col.3.12 in Eph.4.1-3 gains its particular profile from the admonition to ecumenical unity. The author of Ephesians stresses that the church has a given unity in two ways.[96] It is already appointed once for all by God in Christ and is held fast by the confession;[97] but it is always present to the church and has to be striven for specifically in an ecumenical process of learning.[98] In this context the virtues of humility, gentleness and long-suffering mentioned in 4.2 then mean accepting the otherness of other Christians, communities and churches and allowing them to be what they are, tolerating them and joining with them in looking for unity. Humility is thus the opposite of any form of making oneself an absolute;[99] it is a specifically ecumenical virtue.

(*f*) I Peter, which stands in the Pauline tradition, similarly relates the demand for humility to the community and stresses mutuality when it says in 5.5b,6: 'Clothe yourselves, all of you, with humility towards one another, for "God opposes the proud, but gives grace to the humble". Humble yourselves therefore under the mighty hand of God, that in due time he may exalt you.'[100] However, here this admonition follows a clear instruction to superiority and subordination within the community. On the one hand are the presbyters, who have to tend 'God's flock'. Naturally they are not to be in search of gain and must not rule with force (5.1-4). On the other hand the younger members are admonished to submit to the presbyters (5.5a). So here the author attempts to introduce the tradition of reciprocal humility into a hierarchical structure. But can that really work? Can the demand for humility on the part of those 'above' mean anything other than an admonition to condescension in terms of the Graeco-Roman virtue of rule, πραΰτης/ *clementia*? And in that case will not the Greek meaning of ταπεινοφρο-σύνη also be determinative for those 'below' – only now understood in a positive sense – in an inversion of values?[101]

3. '...to bow the neck and take up the position of obedience.'
'Humility' as obedient submission to a hierarchical order

The requirement of humility plays an important role in the letter from the Roman community to that in Corinth at the end of the first century, which is known as I Clement.[102] It is closely related to the situation in Corinth, on which the Roman letter comments. In Corinth a number of presbyters had been dismissed from office by the community on the prompting of a few younger members. The aim of the letter is to restore the deposed presbyters to office and to exile those who engineered their deposition. Clement also makes use of talk of humility to this end. I shall be examining the most important passages in which he speaks of 'humility'.[103]

He mentions it first of all in 2.1 when he describes the once good state of the Corinthian community: 'And you were all humble-minded (ἐταπεινοφρονεῖτε) and in no wise arrogant, yielding subjection rather than demanding it.' 'Humility' as a virtue worth striving for is characterized here above all by its association with the submission of the individual.[104]

If in 2.1 the question to whom the submission is to be made is still left open, the reference to the situation emerges increasingly clearly in the section 13.1-19.1, in which the theme of humility is dominant. The section begins with the invitation 'Let us, therefore, be humble-minded (ταπεινοφρονήσωμεν).' This admonition is to be observed by setting aside the vices of arrogance and conceit, in which showing off is mentioned in first place. Instead of this, it is important to boast in the Lord, who taught gentleness (ἐπιείκεια) and longsuffering (μακροθυμία). After v.2 has cited relevant words of the Lord, in v.3 a humble disposition is then defined as obedience towards him. So here obedience appears alongside the submission of the individual (2.1) as a closer definition of humility.[105] Clement takes up the category of obedience again in 14.1, in a passage which has a reference to the situation in Corinth. It is regarded as 'right and holy' 'to obey God rather than to follow those who in pride and unruliness are the instigators of an abominable jealousy'. Alongside the 'boastfulness'[106] which has already been mentioned, and which of course is the opposite of humility, is now set 'sedition', the term used by Clement to describe the deposition of some presbyters in Corinth. Thus submission to the presbyters appointed in the past is presented as obedience to God. 'Humility' here is obediently taking one's place in the hierarchical order of the community determined by the ministers. Clement clarifies this view of things in 14.2 when he describes those who engineered the deposition of the presbyters as people who 'rush into strife and sedition' and thus alienate themselves 'from right and good order'. So the *status quo* may not be changed.

In chapter 15 Clement promises the deposed presbyters peace negotiations and dismisses as hypocrisy the peace overtures of the 'rebels', which he evidently cannot ignore. In 16.1 he accuses them of having set themselves up over 'the flock of Christ'. The mere act of causing the deposition of some presbyters by the community is regarded as setting themselves up in such a way. They are not accused of having forced their way into the leadership group nor was that the case. They are contrasted with the 'humble-minded' (ταπεινοφρονοῦντες) to whom Christ belongs. The latter are therefore those who submit to the existing authorities. In 16.2 Jesus himself is introduced as 'humble-minded' (ταπεινοφρῶν) and the quotations from Isa.53.1-12 and Ps.21.7-9 (LXX) in 16.3-16 are meant to substantiate this. Verse 17 draws conclusions from this: 'For if the Lord was thus humble-minded, what shall we do, who through him have come under the yoke of his grace?' Whereas according to Phil.2 the humiliation of Christ was the basis for comprehensive solidarity, and therefore the humility of Christians could only be reciprocal, here it becomes willingly taking one's place in the hierarchy; 'the yoke of Christ's grace' becomes specific for those who bear it in recognition of and in obedience towards the authority of those who govern the community and who cannot be deposed.

In chs.17 and 18 Clement gives examples of humility from the history of Israel in which he describes Abraham specifically as 'of humble disposition' (17.2) and in 19.1 sums up all the instances as follows: 'The humility and obedient submission of so many men of such great fame have rendered better not only us, but also the generations before us.' The category of obedience which is reintroduced here is in no way suggested by the examples given earlier.[107] The fact that Clement nevertheless mentions it in this summary suggests that it is the important thing for him; humility is demonstrated in obedience – towards the official authority of the presbyters.

30.1-8 is meant to describe the holiness of the community. That happens first of all in v.1 with the introduction of a catalogue of vices which are to be avoided. It is striking here that within an otherwise traditional series the term νεωτερισμοί occurs, which is not otherwise to be found in earliest Christian literature. The nature of the arrogance which is mentioned in last place is certainly also determined by these 'outbursts of a revolutionary disposition'.[108] The quotation from

Prov.3.34 which is given as a reason in v.2, that God resists the arrogant but is gracious to the humble, is thus cited against the revolutionary action in Corinth which is seen as arrogance. In the face of this, according to v.3 it is important to join 'those to whom grace is given by God'. With reference to the situation in Corinth, here grace can only mean the grace of office. If according to the following admonition harmony is to be achieved by a humble distinction, in turn this can only mean subordination to the authority of the office. The same is true for v.8 at the end of the section, where gentleness, humility and meekness form the positive counterpart to 'frowardness, arrogance and boldness'.

In 56.1 Clement enjoins his readers to pray for the 'rebels' who live in sin, 'that meekness and humility be given to them, that they may submit, not to us, but to the will of God'.[109] Gentleness and humility here are the presupposition for obedient subjection to authority and then certainly also its expression.

Towards the end of his letter Clement first describes the conduct in generalized admonitions and compares it to the atttude of the Fathers who 'were humble-minded ($\tau\alpha\pi\epsilon\iota\nuo\phi\rho o\nuo\hat{\upsilon}\nu\tau\epsilon\varsigma$) towards God, the Father and Creator, and towards all men' (62.2). He then states clearly what he regards as 'seemly': 'to bow the neck, and take up the position of obedience, so that ceasing from vain sedition we may gain without any fault the goal set before us in truth' (63.1). Clement has thus once again given evocative expression to what he understands by obedience: it is unconditional submission to those in authority.[110]

'God makes his will known to us... through authority. The legitimate authorities have the power and duty to direct their subordinates in the place of God; therefore their commands, prohibitions, decisions, wishes and admonitions contain the will of God. Obedience is the simplest, easiest and most certain means of knowing the will of God at any time' (Franz Sinner, *Demut, die Grundtugend des christlichen Lebens*, Wiesbaden 1925, 250). 'Humility and obedience are inseparable but different. Humility is the root and soul of obedience; obedience is the expression and one of the most prominent exercises and effects of humility' (ibid., 255). 'The virtue of obedience is an inclination of the will taken over by the Holy Spirit, to obey the lawful authorities as the representatives of God' (ibid., 256).

'The social principles of Christianity preach cowardice, self-contempt, humiliation, subservience, humility, in short all the properties of the *canaille*, and the proletariat, which does not want to be treated as the *canaille*, needs its courage, its own feelings, its pride and its independence far more than its bread. The social principles of Christianity are lily-livered, and the proletariat is revolutionary' (Karl Marx, 'The Communism of the

Rheinischer Beobachter', Marx-Engels Werke 4, 191-203; 5 September 1847, 200).

The fact that Clement attaches a positive value to humility should not mislead us into assuming that the content in his use of the term matches the Old Testament-Jewish tradition.[111] The situation is more complicated than that. Clement certainly knows this tradition, as he is familiar with the Septuagint.[112] That may have made possible his positive view of the concept of humility. But for its content we need to turn to the wisdom tradition. The substantive and social dimension of the concept which corresponds to a perception 'from below' has completely disappeared. 'Humility' is no longer, as in Paul, a condition of the possibility of a community in solidarity, but is made to serve the development and establishment of hierarchical structures. In view of the situation in Corinth Clement adopts a standpoint 'from above',[113] namely within the leadership of the community. Over against that humility becomes an attitude of subservience. In terms of content that is basically the Graeco-Roman concept of humility, which is used positively merely in a 'inversion of values'.

V

Conclusion
'...among the crosses of the oppressed'

This last section is not intended to offer a 'summary'. In it, rather, I shall attempt to select one particular aspect and take it further. At the end of the last section it had become clear that 'humility' in the sense of obedient subservience emerges only at the periphery of earliest Christianity, in I Clement. But it is this understanding of 'humility' which has had the most powerful effect in church history. In connection with this it is certainly no coincidence that the cross of Jesus has no role in I Clement and that later it even became a symbol of lordship. In view of this influence Heinrich Heine can speak of 'that religion' – here he was referring specifically to Catholicism – which 'became the best-tried support of despotism by its doctrine of the reprehensibility of all earthly goods, the command to canine subservience and the patience of the angels'.[1]

Over against this it is important to recall the other practice of 'humility' shown by Jesus and the majority of primitive Christianity, and its origins which go far back into the Old Testament-Jewish tradition, according to which 'humility' is not a virtue of subjects, but denotes the solidarity of the humiliated. The possibility of this kind of 'humility' in primitive Christianity is specifically based on christology: the cross of Jesus, the utmost shame and humiliation, is taken up and seen positively as the self-identification of the God who promises. His promise to the lowly and humiliated through the prophets, in the Psalms, in non-canonical Jewish writings and through Jesus himself is manifested and concentrated in his cross. As God here is at the same time defined as the one who raised Jesus from the dead, this opens up a future to the humiliated and the oppressed. It is no coincidence that this line has been discovered and is being taken up in Latin American liberation theology and black theology. The humiliated and oppressed can acknowledge their own identity; they need not orientate themselves on prevailing standards – which are the standards of the rulers – but practise a life in solidarity. In their own orientation on the cross of Christ, in deliberate acceptance of the suffering that is forced on them, there begins a process of creative liberation which seeks not just conversion but true humanity for the oppressed, and sisterhood and brotherhood for all.

The perspective I am summarizing here can be filled out by quotations from a book by the South African Takatso A.Mofokeng, *The Crucified among the Crossbearers*.[2] 'The victims of oppression and exploitation start to cut off the knots that ties them to the white man and his white value system as their referential poles. In doing this they become subejcts that do no react but respond to the situation that surrounds them. The consciousness of the black man is no longer submerged in this material situation. It transcends and confronts this situation. As he confronts this situation, he gains a clearer understanding of the situation' (13).[3] By the way in which black Christians celebrate Good Friday in South Africa Mofokeng recognizes that 'In fact it is their own painful life story that they are reliving and narrating. Jesus of Nazareth is tortured, abused and humilated and crucified in them. They are hanging on the cross as innocent victims of white evil forces. Jesus' cry of abandonment is their own daily cry... There is an identification between Jesus' suffering and their suffering' (28). Mofokeng notes the remarkable fact that over against this the resurrection of Jesus 'falls outside the sphere of such intensive celebration because it falls outside the life experience of the average black Christian' (29). So he asks: 'How can these black Christians who are victims of oppression and exploitation reflect on the history of Jesus of Nazareth, especially his resurrection, in such a way that they are moved to seek life in a struggle against forces that deny and destroy life?' (29). He answers this question by understanding 'the cross and resurrection event' as 'a living paradigmatic event for the liberation effort of the oppressed'. 'They had to follow in the footsteps of Jesus of Nazareth. Just like in the case of Jesus, suffering as an ultimate act of historical love becomes power beyond words. It is real suffering but will not be in vain. It will not only be ultimately crowned with victory. It is itself victory over fear and self-preservation, and over all forces, "physical forces in life that are able to effect death" (M.Buthelezi)' (39f.). 'God participates in their struggle which is his struggle. In other words, the history of Jesus goes on in the struggle of the oppressed who rise to affirm themselves... The event of the resurrection of Jesus of Nazareth sustains the struggling community of the oppressed during their protracted hanging on the cross, affirming black humanity and raising a new humanity and a new world in which human life will be possible for all' (41).[4] On the cross of Jesus 'God solidarizes with suffering humankind to the deepest point' (261). In doing this, however, God also indicates the place of those who confess him: 'Historically our locale for our life of engagement, just as his own, is among the crosses of the oppressed. It is from within this locale that our hope for liberation emerges and becomes credible and the deeper we descend into this deep locale of the crosses, the nearer our resurrection' (98).

Alongside this last quotation from Mofokeng I would set a poem by Reiner Kunze:

On Calvary Hill near Retz in January

The vine too is crucified
bent forward naked
arms bound outstretched
the very gesture of the redeemer
on the sandstone cross
And *blood and water* become grape
from which year by year they harvest the sweet abundant wine
As from the stone of faith
So many crucified on the way to the one[5]

It is important for those who are not numbered among the humiliated to learn and practise humility as solidarity with the humiliated. That would be an ecumenical virtue fundamentally different from patronizing condescension. Gustavo Gutíerrez mentions a Bolivian farmworker who said at Puebla: 'An atheist is someone who fails to practise justice towards the poor.'[6]

Abbreviations

Bibliography

Alföldy, Geza, 'Die Freilassung von Sklaven und die Struktur der Sklaverei in
    der römischen Kaiserzeit', in *Sozial- und Wirtschaftsgeschichte der römischen
    Kaiserzeit*, ed. Helmut Schneider, WdF 552, Darmstadt 1981, 336-71
– , *Römische Sozialgeschichte*, Wiesbaden ²1979
Arvedson, Tomas, *Das Mysterium Christi. Eine Studie zu Mt 11,25-30*, Uppsala
    1937
Awerbuch, Marianne, 'Demut II, Judentum', *TRE* VII, 1981, 462f.
Bammel, Ernst, πτωχός κτλ, *TDNT* 6, 888-915
Berger, Klaus, 'Wissenssoziologie und Exegese', *Kairos* 19, 1977, 124-33
Birkeland, Harris, ani *und* anaw *in den Psalmen*, Oslo 1933
– , *Die Feinde des Individuums in der israelitischen Psalmenliteratur. Ein Beitrag
    zur Kenntnis der semitischen Literatur- und Religionsgeschichte*, Oslo 1933
– , *The Evildoers in the Book of Psalms*, Oslo 1955
Boer, Willem den, '*Tapeinos* in Pagan and Christian Terminology', in *Tria
    corda. Scritti in onore di Arnaldo Momigliano*, ed. E.Gabba, Como 1983,
    143-62
Brox, Norbert, *Der erste Petrusbrief*, EKK XXI, 1979
Brunner, Gerbert, *Die theologische Mitte des ersten Klemensbriefs. Ein Beitrag
    zur Hermeneutik frühchristlicher Texte*, FTS 11, 1972
Bultmann, Rudolf, καυχάομαι κτλ, *TDNT* 3, 646-54
Burchard, Christoph, 'Gemeinde in der strohernen Epistel. Mutmassungen
    über Jakobus', in *Kirche. FS Günther Bornkamm*, ed. Dieter Lührmann and
    Georg Strecker, Tübingen 1980, 315-28
Christ, Felix, *Jesus Sophia. Die Sophia-Christologie bei den Synoptikern*,
    ATANT 57, 1970
Crüsemann, Frank, 'Die unveränderbare Welt. Überlegungen zur Krisis der
    Weisheit beim Prediger (Kohelet)', in *Der Gott der kleinen Leute. Sozialge-
    schichtliche Bibelauslegungen 1. Altes Testament*, ed. Willy Schottroff and
    Wolfgang Stegemann, Munich and Gelnhausen, etc. 1979, 80-104
Dibelius, Martin, *Der Brief des Jakobus*, KEK 15, edited with a supplement by
    Heinrich Greeven, ¹¹1964
Dihle, Albrecht, 'Demut', *RAC* III, 1957, 735-78
Ebach, Jürgen, 'Arme und Armut im Alten Testament. Zum Umgang mit
    alttestamentlichen Aussagen', *ZMiss* 5, 1979, 143-53
– , *Ursprung und Ziel. Erinnerte Zukunft und erhoffte Vergangenheit. Biblische
    Exegesen, Reflexionen, Geschichten*, Neukirchen-Vluyn 1986
– , 'Das Recht der Armen', in *Die Mülltonnen der Reichen und der arme
    Lazarus*, ed. Hartwig Liebich, Stuttgart 1982, 17-21
Elliger, Karl, *Das Buch der zwölf Kleinen Propheten* II. *Die Propheten Nahum,
    Habakuk, Zephanja, Haggai, Sacharja, Maleachi*, ATD 25, ⁴1959
– , *Studien zum Habakuk – Kommentar vom Toten Meer*, BHT 15, 1953
Esser, Hans-Helmut, 'Demut/ταπεινός', *TBLNT* I, ⁴1977, 176-9

Fabry, H.-J., 'dal', TWAT II, 1977, 221-44

Farris, Stephen, The Hymns of Luke's Infancy Narratives. Their Origin, Meaning and Significance, JSNTS Supplement Series 9, Sheffield 1985

Fendler, Marlene, 'Zur Sozialkritik des Amos. Versuch einer wirtschafts- und sozialgeschichtlicher Interpretation alttestamentlicher Texte', EvTh 33, 1973, 32-53

Foerster, Werner, ἁρπάζω, ἁρπαγμός, TDNT I, 471-4

Frey, Christofer, 'Tugenden – ein Thema für evangelische Ethik?', EvErz 37, 1985, 349-59

Giesen, Heinz, 'ταπεινός κτλ', EWNT III, 1983, 798-804

Gnilka, Joachim, Der Philipperbrief, HTK I, X 3, ²1976

– , Das Matthäusevangelium, 1, HTK I 1, 1986

Grundmann, Walter, Das Evangelium nach Matthäus, THK I ³1972

– , ταπεινός κτλ, TDNT 8, 1-27

Hauck, Friedrich, and Siegfried Schulz, πραΰς, πραΰτης, TDNT 6, 645-51

Hempel, Johannes, Das Ethos des Alten Testaments, BZAW 67, ²1964

Hengel, Martin, Judaism and Hellenism, London and Philadelphia 1974

Herrmann, Siegfried, A History of Israel in Old Testament Times, London and Philadelphia ²1981

Hock, Ronald F., 'Paul's Tentmaking and the Problem of His Social Class', JBL 97, 1978, 555-64

Hofius, Otfried, Der Christushymnus Philipper 2,6-11. Untersuchungen zur Gestalt und Aussage eines urchristlichen Psalms, WUNT 17, 1976

Jacob, Edmond, 'ψυχή κτλ B. The Anthropology of the Old Testament', TDNT IX, 614-29

Jens, Walter, Am Anfang der Stall, am Ende der Galgen: Jesus von Nazareth (seine Geschichte nach Matthäus), Stuttgart 1972

Jeremias, Gert, Der Lehrer der Gerechtigkeit, SUNT 2, 1963

Käsemann, Ernst, 'Kritische Analyse von Phil.2,5-11', in Exegetische Versuche und Besinnungen I, Göttingen 1960, 51-95

– , Commentary on Romans, Grand Rapids and London ²1982

Kaiser, Otto, Isaiah 1-12, OTL, London and Philadelphia 1983

Keel, Othmar, Feinde und Gottesleugner. Studien zum Image der Widersacher in den Individualpsalmen, SBS 7, 1969

Kellermann, Ulrich, Messias und Gesetz. Grundlinien einer alttestamentlichen Heilserwartung. Eine traditionsgechichtliche Einführung, BS 61, 1971

Kippenberg, Hans G., 'Die Entlassung aus Schuldknechtschaft im antiken Judäa. Eine Legitimitätsvorstellung von Verwandtschaftsgruppen', in Vor Gott sind alle gleich. Soziale Gleichheit, soziale Ungleichheit und die Religionen, ed. Günter Kehrer, Düsseldorf 1983, 74-104

Klostermann, Erich, Das Matthausevangelium, HNT 4, ⁴1971

Koch, Klaus, 'Die Entstehung der sozialen Kritik bei den Profeten', in Probleme biblischer Theologie. FS Gerhard von Rad, ed. Hans Walter Wolff, Munich 1971, 236-57

Kraus, Hans-Joachim, Psalmen 1, BK XV 1, ²1961

Lang, Bernhard, 'Prophetie und Ökonomie im alten Israel', in Vor Gott sind *alle gleich. Soziale Gleichheit, soziale Ungleichheit und die Religionen*, ed. Günter Kehrer, Düsseldorf 1983, 53-73

– , 'Sklaven und Unfreie im Buch Amos', *VT* 31, 1981, 482-8

– , 'Wie wird man Prophet in Israel', in id., *Wie wird man Prophet in Israel? Aufsätze zum Alten Testament*, Düsseldorf 1980, 31-58

Lichtenberger, Hermann, *Studien zum Menschenbild in Texten der Qumrangemeinde*, SUNT 15, 1980

Lietzmann, Hans, *An die Korinther* I.II, HNT 9, [4]1949

Lohfink, Norbert, 'Von der "Anawim-Partei" zur "Kirche der Armen". Die bibelwissenschaftliche Ahnentafel eines Hauptbegriffs der "Theologie der Befreiung"', *Bib* 67, 1986, 153-76

Lohse, Eduard, *Colossians and Philemon*, Hermeneia, Philadelphia 1981

Martin-Achard, R., '*'nh* II elend sein', *THAT* II, 1976, 342-50

Martino, Francesco de, *Wirtschaftsgeschichte des alten Rom*, Munich 1985

Mehl, Roger, 'Demut IV. Systematisch', *RGG*[3] II, 1958, 80-2.

Mussner, Franz, *Der Jakobusbrief*, HTK XIII 1, [3]1975

Nickelsburg, George W.E., 'The Apocalyptic Message of I Enoch 92-105', *CBQ* 39, 1977, 309-28

– , 'Riches, the Rich, and God's Judgment in I Enoch 92-105 and the Gospel according to Luke', *NTS* 25, 1979, 324-44

Percy, Ernst, *Die Botschaft Jesu. Eine traditionskritische und exegetische Untersuchung*, Lund 1953

Pflaum, Hans-Georg, 'Das Römische Kaiserreich', *PWG* IV, 1963, 317-428

Plöger, Otto, *Sprüche Salomos (Proverbia)*, BK XVII, 1984

Preuss, Horst-Dietrich, 'Demut I. Altes Testament', *TRE* VIII, 1981, 459-61

Rad, Gerhard von, *Old Testament Theology*, II *The Theology of Israel's Prophetic Traditions*, Edinburgh 1965 reissued London 1975

Radler, Aleksander, 'Demut. VIII, Ethisch', *TRE* VIII, 1981, 483-8

Rehrl, Stefan, 'Demut III. Neues Testament, IV. Alte Kirche', *TRE* VIII, 1981, 463-8

– , *Das Problem der Demut in der profan-griechisch Literature im Vergleich zu Septuaginta und Neuem Testament*, AeC 4, 1961

Rudolph, Wilhelm, *Joel, Amos, Obadja, Jona*, KAT XIII 2, 1971

– , *Micha, Nahum, Habakuk, Zephanja*, KAT XIII 3, 1975

Ruppert, Lothar, *Der leidende Gerechte. Eine motivgeschichtliche Untersuchung zum Alten Testament und zwischentestamentlichen Judentum*, FzB 5, 1972

Sacchi, Paolo, 'Henochgestalt/Henochliteratur', *TRE* XV, 1986, 42-54

Sauer, Georg, *Jesus Sirach (Ben Sira)*, JSHRZ III/5. 1981, 479-644

Schlatter, Adolf, *Der Evangelist Matthäus. Seine Sprache, sein Ziel, seine Selbständigkeit*, Stuttgart [2]1933

Schlier, Heinrich, 'Die Eigenart der christlichen Mahnung nach dem Apostel Paulus', in id., *Mitarbeiter der Schöpfung. Bibel und Arbeitswelt*, ed. Luise and Willy Schottroff, Munich 1983, 149-206

– , 'Das Magnificat und die älteste Tradition über Jesus von Nazareth', *EvTh* 38, 1978, 298-313

Schottroff, Luise, and Wolfgang Stegemann, *Jesus von Nazareth – Hoffnung der Armen*, Stuttgart et al. 1978

66   Humility: Solidarity of the Humiliated

Schottroff, Willy, 'Der Prophet Amos. Versuch der Würdigung seines Auftretens unter sozialgeschichtlichem Aspekt', in *Der Gott der kleinen Leute. Sozialgeschichtliche Bibelauslegungen 1.Altes Testament*, ed. id. and Wolfgang Stegemann, Munich and Gelnhausen 1979, 39-66

Schrage, Wolfgang, *The Ethics of the New Testament*, Philadelphia 1987 and Edinburgh 1988

– , 'Der Jakobusbrief', in Horst Balz and id., *Die 'Katholischen' Briefe*, NTD 10, ²1980, 5-59

Schürmann, Heinz, *Das Lukasevangelium*, I, *1,1-9,50*, HTK III 1, 1969

Schwantes, Milton, *Das Recht der Armen*, Beiträge zur biblischen Exegese und Theologie 4, Frankfurt 1977

Schweitzer, Eduard, *Good News according to Matthew*, Atlanta and London 1976

– , 'ψυχή κτλ D.New Testament', *TDNT* 9, 635-57

Stegemann, Hartmut, *Die Enstehung der Qumrangemeinde*, Bonn dissertation 1971

Theissen, Gerd, 'Christologie und soziale Erfahrung. Wissenssoziologische Aspekte paulinischer Christologie', in id., *Studien zur Soziologie des Urchristentums*, WUNT 19, ²1983, 318-30

Uhlig, Siegbert, *Das äthiopische Henochbuch*, JSHRZ V 6, 1984, 461-780

Vielhauer, Philipp, *Geschichte der urchristlichen Literatur. Einleitung in das Neue Testament, die Apokryphen und die Apostolischen Väter*, Berlin and New York 1975

Weiser, Artur, *Das Buch Jeremia*, ATD 20,21, ⁶1969

– , *Introduction to the Old Testament*, London 1971

Weiss, Konrad, φέρω κτλ, *TDNT* 9, 57-89

Wengst, Klaus, *Pax Romana and the Peace of Jesus Christ*, London and Philadelphia 1987

– , 'Versöhnung und Befreiung. Ein Aspekt des Themas "Schuld und Vergebung" im Lichte des Kolosserbriefes', *EvTh* 36, 1976, 14-26

Wiedemann, Thomas, 'The Regularity of Manumission at Rome', *Classical Quarterly* 35, 1985, 162-75

Wilckens, Ulrich, *Der Brief an die Römer*, 3, *Röm. 12-16*, EKK VI 3, 1982

Wildberger, Hans, *Jesaja 3. Jesaja 28-39. Das Buch, der Prophet und seine Botschaft*, BK X 3, 1982

Winkler, Klaus, 'Clementia', *RAC* III, 1957, 206-31

Wolff, Hans-Walter, *Joel und Amos*, Hermeneia, Philadelphia 1977

Notes

I. *Introduction: 'It is always the secure who are humble'*

1. Rehrl, 'Demut', 464.
2. Grundmann, ταπεινός, 11f.
3. Esser, 176.
4. Dihle, 741; cf. 749.
5. Mehl, 80: cf. also the continuation of the quotation: 'The humiliated person is primarily the one who is subjected, who bows the knee to his victor and prostrates himself on the ground... If a legal order replaces the old order of violence, it is the social hierarchy which makes use of humility as a point of reference.' That comes at the beginning of an article which discusses 'humility' from the standpoint of systematic theology. By contrast a more recent article on the ethical aspect does not do justice to this dimension and understands 'humility' only under the wider concept of virtue: Radler, 483-8, esp. 483f.
6. That is not to claim that I am doing this for the first time, but an attempt should be made to do it with some consistency.
7. It is impossible to give all the evidence within the limits of this book, nor shall I attempt to do so. Particularly in the first two parts I have cited only a small selection of texts. But they should be enough to make it possible to follow the question that has been asked. See also Rehrl, 'Demut', and the articles by Grundmann, Esser, Dihle, Martin-Achard, Preuss, Awerbuch and Giesen (see bibliography).
8. He speaks only of the 'New Testament' here (132) but precisely the same is already true of Israel from the time of the liberation from slavery in Egypt.

II. *'Shameful deeds, lowly origin, sordid poverty and mean handiwork'*

1. Dihle, 737. Here he distinguishes from humility the demand, very well known in Greece, 'to know oneself and one's limitations' (738). Rehrl, *Problem*, does not do this and thus comes to another conclusion (cf. above all the end of his book, 196-203). He defines *a priori* the 'Christian concept of humility' (13-23) of which he gives the following summary: 'Humility is that virtue which puts human striving for fulfilment and selfhood in a proper perspective before God and humankind (humility of stage I); in addition, in so far as it is good and permissible (!) it bestows the capacity also to renounce that validity to which a person would have a claim by virtue of his being and status(!) (humility of stage II)' (22). The frontiers of stage II 'lie where the overall order demands that the respect and authority due should not be endangered' (19). In this way a good accord can be arrived at between the Greek fear 'of hybris or self-assertion on the one hand and worthless self-surrender and cringing compliance on the other. The virtue of modesty lies for it half-way between these two vices. That is also true of Christians' (201).

2. The words concerned are ταπεινός and *humilis* and their derivatives.

3. Aristides, *Eulogy of Rome*, 18.

4. Caesar, *De Bello Gallico* VII, 54,3. Cf. also IV, 3,4, according to which the Suebi 'made the Ubii tributary to themselves and greatly diminished their strength and importance (*humiliores... redegerunt*)'. According to Plutarch, *Solon* 22,2, in view of the mass of helots living around Sparta Lycurgus thought it better 'for them not to be left idle, but to be kept down (ταπεινοῦσθαι) by constant work and oppression'.

5. Grundmann, 2 (he also gives further passages).

6. Euripides, *Andromache*, 164-8.

7. Seneca, *Epistles* 47.1.

8. Cf. Alföldy, *Sozialgeschichte*, 83-138, especially the diagram on 131.

9. As an example of this I mention only Livy III, 36,7. In this passage Livy speaks of the terror of the Decemvirs which was first of all indiscriminate: 'It gradually began to be directed entirely against the people (*plebs*). They kept away from the patricians and acted arbitrarily and cruelly against the lowly (*humiliores*).'

10. Cicero, *De officiis* II, 70.

11. Cicero, *Letters to Atticus* 7a, 1.

11a. Cf. Friedrich Nietzsche, *Beyond Good and Evil*, Collected Works 12, London 1909, § 260; *On the Genealogy of Morality*, Collected Works 13, London 1910, I, 10.

12. Aristotle, *Politics*, VIII,2,1 (1337b).

13. Pliny, *Epistles*, I,3,3.

14. Homer, *Odyssey* 17, 320-3.

15. Grundmann, 2. Even Dio Chrysostom has Diogenes explain to Alexander that 'none other than his own disposition (νοῦς) is man's spirit (δαίμων); that the spirit of the understanding and good man is good, that of the evil man is evil, and similarly that of a free man is free, that of a slave servile, that of a kingly and high-minded man royal, that of a lowly and ignoble man humble (ταπεινός)' (4,80).

16. Cf. the 'mood' in the fictitious account of a blow of fate in Homer, *Odyssey* 17, 419-44.

17. Livy, XXII, 25, 18f.

18. Livy, XXIII, 3,11.

19. Seneca, *Epistles* 87,15-17.

20. Seneca, *De ira* II, 21,4.

21. Aristotle, *Politics* IV, 9,5 (1295B).

22. Aristotle, *Nicomachean Ethics* IV, 3,26 (1124b).

23. Ibid., I, 10,15 (1101a), and on it Frey, 353: 'Aristotle has ideals of rank and an anthropology which is socially conditioned: generosity, largeness of spirit and high-mindedness (...'a great soul') reflect the men of the upper classes who cultivate themselves.'

24. Aristotle, *Rhetoric* II, 3,1-6 (1380a).

25. For 'mildness' as the virtue of the powerful cf. Hauck/Schulz 646, and nn.4-6; Winkler, 213f. Particular notice should be taken of the explicit separation of πρᾶος and ταπεινός in Dio Cassius 74,5,7, where Emperor Pertinax is

described as a 'majestic being without a gloomy nature, admirable without humility (πρᾶος ἔξω τοῦ ταπεινοῦ), understanding without being under-handed, just without scrupulousness, without niggardliness in carrying out his office, high-minded without arrogant pride.'

26. See n.24.

27. The connection between lowly social status and negative feelings emerges very clearly from a series of concepts in early Stoicism: 'Lowliness, humility (ταπεινότης), slavery, joylessness, lack of courage, wretchedness, any evil situation' (SVF III, 107).

28. Xenophon, *Memorabilia* III, 10,5. Cf. the similar contrasts in Cicero, *Fam.* III, 10,7; *De Divinatione* I, 88. It finds expression in rhetoric when Quintilian defines as prohibited lowly expressions (*humilia*) those which are 'below the status of the objects or rank (viz. of the person)' (*Institutes* VIII, 2,2).

29. Lucian, *Somnium*, 9.

30. Ibid., 13. For contempt especially of sculpture by members of the upper classes cf. also Plutarch, *Pericles* 2.1: 'No generous youth, from seeing the Zeus at Pisa or the Hera at Argos, longs to be Pheidias or Polycleitus.' For the immediate context see p.11 and n.53. The same notion occurs in the continuation of Education's speech in *Somnium* 9: 'Even if you should become a Phidias or a Polycleitus and should create many marvellous works, everyone would praise your craftsmanship, to be sure, but none of those who saw you, if he were sensible, would pray to be like you, for no matter what you might be, you would be considered a mechanic, a man who has naught but his hands, a man who lives by his hands.'

31. In *Somnium* 9, by the addition of τὴν γνώμην, ταπεινός is expressly described as a disposition and thus as being ethical.

32. Lucian, *Somnium*, 11.

33. Ibid., 13. According to Plutarch Cato the Elder used eloquence 'as it were like a second body, in order to attain the good and not just the necessary, as the organ for a man who does not want to live inactively and in humility (ταπεινός)' (*Marcus Cato* 1,4).

34. Lucian, *Somnium*, 18.

35. I would refer once again to Alföldy, *Sozialgeschichte*, 83-138, especially 93-102, 130-8. See also Origen, *Contra Celsum* I, 29: 'Among men noble birth, honourable and distinguished parents, an upbringing at the hands of wealthy people who are able to spend money on the education of their son(!), and a great and famous native country, are things which help to make a man famous and distinguished and get his name well known.'

36. Alföldy had written in his social history, as a result of his article on the freeing of slaves: 'As a rule the slave had the prospect of being freed at the latest when he was about thirty, and was given freedom, if he survived to that age' (121). This theory cannot be maintained in that form; according to de Martino it is 'beyond doubt an exaggeration to say that the majority of slaves received their freedom' (295). For criticism of Alföldy see especially Wiedemann, passim.

37. Alföldy, *Sozialgeschichte*, 121.

38. According to ibid., 135, social decline was 'a rare occurrence under the

consolidated conditions of the early empire. At most only the inhabitants of the provinces in the first generations after their subjection will have been affected to any degree, and the number would steadily decline during the empire. Of course there were always impoverished families and those in debt, especially in the country, who had for example to sell their children as slaves, but the broader classes of the people rarely experienced such a decline.' This description is painted in rather too rosy colours: when the latifundia economy expanded in the early empire, it must necessarily have been at the expense of the smaller landowners.

39. For social mobility in the early empire cf. Theissen, 321-4, and the literature mentioned in nn.6-8, 10, there. Theissen sums up as follows: 'So there were limited chances of upward social mobility. How often they were realized is unimportant. The decisive thing is that men's expectations could be shaped by the fact that everyone in his life could take a step upwards.'

40. See the example of Lucian, mentioned above.

41. Cf. Alföldy, *Sozialgeschichte*, 135: 'Nevertheless the Roman social system offered numerous chances of social ascent, which one could at least strive for; this elasticiity contributed substantially to its strength and stability.'

42. Aristides, *Eulogy of Rome*, 60. For modern imitators of such an ideology cf. Pflaum, 383f.

43. Aristides, *Eulogy of Rome*, 85.

44. Livy, I, 8,5.

45. I would just mention king Servius Tullius, who is said to have been the son of a slave girl (Livy I, 39,3-6; Ovid, *Fasti*, 6,781-4), and the grandfather of Otho, son of a Roman *eques* and a 'woman of lower station; perhaps not even freeborn', who became a senator (Suetonius, *Otho* 1,1). Juvenal finds it difficult not to write satires 'when with all the aristocrats one has become rich who in my youth scraped my beard' (I, 24f.; cf. X, 225f.).

46. Quintilian, *Institutes* III, 7,10.

47. Tacitus, *Agricola* 16,4.

48. Pliny, *Epistles*, VIII, 24,6.

49. Ibid., VIII, 6,15.

50. Dio Chrysostom, 2,75f.

51. Pliny, *Panegyricus*, 4,5.

52. As an example he mentions, for instance: 'We take a delight in perfumes and dyes, but dyers and perfumers we regard as illiberal and vulgar folk' (Plutarch, *Pericles*, 1,4).

53. Plutarch, *Pericles*, 2,1. The quotation given in n.30 follows.

54. Plutarch, *Moralia* 1b,c. Plutarch speaks similarly of Perseus when he accuses him of 'littleness and baseness of character', and continues that he is not a legitimate child but was the child of a seamstress (*Aemilius* 8,6). But he has to go on to accord him a degree of boldness, 'although he was ignoble and mean' (9,1).

55. Plutarch, *Moralia*, 554f-555a. Cf. also 807e of Agesilaus: 'extremely weak and of a humble disposition' (ἀσθενέστατος καὶ ταπεινότατος).

56. Plutarch, *Moralia*, 336e.

57. Plutarch, *Moralia*, 475e; cf. also the contrast between 'insignificant,

subservient (ταπεινός) and ignoble' with 'self-confidence, free spirit, ambition and generosity' in 762e; further 64e.

58. Plutarch, *Moralia*,599b. Cf. also Diogenes Laertius I, 93: 'Do not be arrogant in prosperity: if you fall into poverty, do not humble yourself. Know how to bear the changes of fortune with humility.' In another passage he says of Zeus, 'He is humbling the proud and exalting the humble' (Diogenes Laertius I, 69; cf. also Hesiod, *Works and Days*, 3-8). The intention of this is not to be thought to be an egalitarian society; the background is the experience of upward and downward social mobility, interpreted as changes of fortune. Both passages are cited by den Boer (148), for his article see n.82 below.

59. Plutarch, *Moralia*, 336e.

60. Plutarch, *Moralia*, 475e.

61. In *Moralia* 824e, Plutarch explains that it is not worth entering into a political contest: 'For what dominion, what fame is there for those who are victorious? What sort of power is it which a small edict of a proconsul may annul or transfer to another man?'

62. Seneca, *Epistles* 74.28, cf. 30: 'The wise man is not distressed by the loss of children or of friends. For he endures their death in the same spirit in which he awaits his own. And he fears the one as little as he grieves for the other.'

63. Seneca, *De vita beata* 25,4. The continuation goes: 'Nevertheless I prefer to be victor rather than to be taken prisoner.'

64. Seneca, *Epistles* 115,6. 7 depicts the opposite, seeing wickedness despite the blinding light which emanates from riches, offices and power. Cf. also Dio Chrysostom 15.29: 'We shall have to concede that a large number of so-called slaves have the dispositions of free men, and a large number of freeborn men have the disposition of slaves', and the wider context as far as 32.

65. Seneca, *Epistles* 66,3.

66. Ibid. 68,2. Cf. *ad Marciam de consolatione*, 26.4. The dead father says from his 'place in heaven' (26.1), 'Nothing that is, as you think, desirable, nothing that is lofty, nothing glorious, but all is lowly (*humilia*), heavy laden, and troubled, and beholds how small a fraction of the light in which we dwell.'

67. Seneca, *De tranquillitate animi* 10,3. For all men there is liberation only through death, 'death it is in which no one feels the humility of his position' (*ad Marciam de consolatione* 20,2).

68. Seneca, *De tranquillitate animi* 10,4.

69. Seneca, *Epistles*, 123,16.

70. Seneca, *Epistles*, 74,16f.

71. Epictetus, *Dissertationes* IV, 7,7f.

72. Ibid., 9-11.

73. Ibid., III, 24,56. Cf. also I,3,4: 'All those who think that by their birth they are called to fidelity, to self-respect and to unerring judgment in the use of external impressions, cherish no mean or ignoble (ταπεινόν) thoughts about themselves.' Also IV, 1.1-5; Cicero, *Tusc.* V, 29f.; Marcus Aurelius, IX, 40,5.

74. Plutarch, *Moralia*, 549d.

75. For this passage see also Grundmann 3, with n.4 against Rehrl.

76. Plutarch, *Moralia*, 548e.

77. Statius, *Achilleis* 1,144. In this context Virgil, *Aeneid* 12,930 could be

cited, where the defeated Turnus 'looks up at Aeneas, humble and weeping, and raises his right hand in petition'.

78. Propertius III, 17,1.

79. Dio Chrysostom 77/78, 26.

80. Propertius III, 9,29.

81. Xenophon, *Agesilaus* 11,11.

82. *Historia Augusta*, Julian 9,1. Den Boer cites both passages and wants to cite this use *in bonam partem* as a revision of the general view that the terms ταπεινός and *humilis* are used in pagan literature only pejoratively (145). The 'only' must certainly be revised, but the occasional positive use cannot basically change the overall picture.

83. Propertius I, 10, 27f.

III. 'Thou art the God who humblest thyself'

1. For the translation 'because of' cf. Lang, 'Sklaven', 482f.; Kippenberg, 'Entlassung', 81.

2. For a more accurate dating of the prophetic activity of Amos, which is to be assumed 'to have lasted at least a year', between the middle of the reign of Jeroboam II and 760 at the latest, cf. W.Schottroff, 39f.

3. According to W.Schottroff the condition for this was not the rise of Assyria in the east, since real Assyrian expansion began only under Tiglath-pileser I (745 BC); in the time of Jeroboam Assyria had itself been threatened by the new power of Urartu in the north. 'In the Syrian sphere, however, the weakness of Assyria led to new rivalries between the Aramaean states, which had evidently been more favourable to the restitution of Israel's territory than the previous Syrian campaigns of the Assyrians' (48).

4. Herrmann mentions 'the often-repeated judgment that during the time of king Jeroboam II of Israel and Azariah (Uzziah) of Judah there was a lessening of tension, and Israel enjoyed a kind of "Indian summer" before the invasion of the Assyrians under Tiglath-pileser III. This view has been challenged in more recent times' (233).

5. Wolff speaks of 'economic prosperity' and mentions as its other side 'social upheaval. The rich became richer while the poor become poorer. Such early capitalism quickly led to expropriation of the holdings of the smaller landowners' (89f.). For the economic and social development see also Fendler, 34f. For the time of Jeroboam II she finally notes: 'At this time the traditional social structure was undermined to such a degree that the discrepancy between traditional self-understanding and changed social praxis brought about a crisis in consciousness which found its contemporary expression throughout the proclamation of Amos' (35). Herrmann sums up the economic features of the era of the Jehu dynasty as follows: 'The original agricultural system, which was essentially one of smallholdings, was overlaid by a growing pattern of estates and large-scale agriculture which was developed with royal support' (239).

6. Cf.W.Schottroff, 49f.

7. Cf. Lang, 'Prophetie', 60-2; W.Schottroff, 50f.

8. Cf. Koch, 243.

9. Lang, 'Prophetie', 55.

10. 'Depending on the level of the debt... the debtors could soon become "tenants" on their own lands as a result of regular provision of pledges, working more for others than for themselves' (Fendler, 360); cf. Lang, 'Prophetie', 62f.

11. 'The stated reason for this selling of human beings was to satisfy creditors demanding monetary compensation for "silver" owed them, or even in lieu of other payment for a mere "pair of sandals" (which had been stolen or borrowed and then lost?)' (Wolff, 165), cf. Fendler, 49.

12. Lang, 'Sklaven', 483; id., 'Prophetie', 63.

13. 'As an outsider sees it, the poor buy grain from the dealer, but in reality the dealer is buying his customers, i.e. making them permanent debtors... The poor cannot pay for the goods they have bought for food or as seed, become debtors and owe interest, and finally end up in that servile dependence whch is characteristic of the capitalist system' (Lang, 'Prophetie', 63f.). For slavery for debt see also Kippenberg, passim, esp. 81: 'As in other ancient societies, so in Israel slavery for debt was the favourite means by which the rich appropriated goods and human beings'; and 86: 'The discrepancy between the loan taken on and the consequences for the debtor who failed to pay was notorious. In the legal system relating to debt there was no comparison between the value of a loan which was given to a poor farmer to see him over to the next harvest and the years of slavery whch would follow any failure to pay.' Cf. also Fendler, 38-40. The statement in 2.7 ('Son and father go to in the same maid') refers to 'a girl enslaved for debt who belongs to the household and the family and is made sexually available to both the paterfamilias and his son' (Fendler, 42); cf. also Rudolph, 142f.

14. Lang, 'Sklaven', 484-6; id., 64f.

15. Cf. the passage 8.5 quoted above, together with 5.12 and Fendler, 43f.; W.Schottroff, 52f.

16. 'It is striking that Amos... often criticizes those who formally have right on their side' (Ebach, 'Arme', 143). 'The old laws which essentially presuppose a society of free farmers, structured in families and clans, no longer hold. The powerful succeed in changing the social order even more in their favour, not by breaking the laws but largely with the support of the laws. Laws which presuppose equality help to make the already existing inequality even worse' (ibid., 150).

17. Koch, 244.

18. For the dating see the discussion in Wildberger, 1137f.

19. Wildberger, 1142.

20. Fendler writes of the women of Samaria, compared by Amos in 4.1 with fat cows, and their life of luxury: 'They are as accustomed as is the fine cow to the best possible care and, like the cow, interested only in their usual food – not in how it is made possible. But that is what Amos is concerned with' (47).

21. Fabry's categorical remark that 'there is no evidence of class struggle in the Old Testament' (231) is just an assertion resting on an ideological prejudice. Some pages later he himself mentions aspects of the class struggle from above when he instances as the 'background' to Amos' prophecy: 'an unsocial quest for expansion on the part of the great landowners, the stewards of the royal

domains... a degree of systematization in actions against the smallholder; unashamed demands for what is due (5.11) – the prevention of legal actions and claims for redress by bribing the judge and turning the law to their own advantage... – finally selling those who are exploited in this way into slavery for debt' (236). For the description of Amos' situation I follow above all Lang, 'Prophetie', 459-66, and Koch, 242-5, who presuppose antagonism between the upper classes living in the towns and the smallholders in the country. This seems to me to fit the texts better than the picture of society outlined by Fendler (49-52). She assumes middle classes who on the one hand are exposed to the pressure from above and on the other hand pass it on. 'This ambivalence which appears in the middle classes prevents us from speaking clearly of levels of exploiter and exploited' (52). But her argument that according to 2.6 'debtors and creditors live in relatively modest circumstances' is based on a literal understanding of 'sandals' as an 'indication of the trivial size of the debt' (49). And it is very improbable that in 2.8 the creditors should be said to be relatively poor and then in the same sentence 'well-to-do or even rich' (49f.). Of course we cannot rule out differentiations and transitions, but what shapes society is the fundamental contrast between the upper class in the city and the smallholder in the country.

22. Cf. also W.Schottroff, 52, who speaks of the 'impoverishment and oppression of large strata of the people' as the 'price' of the riches on the other side.

23. W.Schottroff, 41; cf. there the whole section on Amos' profession.

24. Amos is to be understood to be arguing here 'that he does not need to be a *nabi* (a professional prophet) to support himself, because he has sufficient income' (Rudolph, 256).

25. Against Lang, 'Prophetie', 66, who without beating about the bush makes Amos a 'landowner' and assigns him to the 'propertied upper class'; cf. also 70. At another point he speaks of him as a 'rich owner of flocks' ('Prophet', 40).

26. That is true even if we do not think, as usual, of the Tekoa in Judah near to Bethlehem but of a 'Galilean Tekoa presupposed in post-biblical times' to which Lang transfers Amos because it would be possible for him to tend sycamore trees there.

27. It seems to me to be worth imagining Amos the 'shepherd' and 'preparer of sycamore figs' as a 'specialist' who in this capacity essentially lives in and travels around the country but also has access to the rich.

28. This bias is not just apparent; against Fendler, 53.

29. Cf. further Isa.41.17: 'When the poor and needy (*hāʿanīyyīm wᵉhā-ʾebyōnīm*/οἱ πτωχοὶ καὶ οἱ ἐνδεεῖς) seek water, and there is none, and their tongue is parched with thirst, I the Lord will answer them, I the God of Israel will not forsake them.'

30. According to W.Schottroff it is a 'basic experience' of Israel 'that Yahweh despises the great... and the strong (...Amos 2.9a), that he is to be found on the side of the weak and the insignificant (...Amos 7.2, 5), in order to give them somewhere to live (cf. Amos 2.9) and the means of living (Amos 7.1-3, 4-6).' Cf. also 58: 'Amos's Yahweh is the God of the small people, the victims who

are ground to pieces without mercy in the economic activities of the Israel of this time.'

31. Lang sees as 'a rational nucleus of the prophetic sermon' the fact that 'war affects the fortified cities with their concentration of political power to an incomparably greater degree than the country and only cities are the source of plunder... The possessions of the city-dweller are plundered and he himself is carried off; the smallholder remains sitting on the land and becomes its owner' ('Prophetie', 68).

32. Cf. also Koch, 256. For the impoverished in the prophecy of Amos cf. also Schwantes, 87-99, and for the parallelism with the 'righteous' which is discussed in the following paragraph see esp. 93.

33. 'Hope is set on a new member of the house of David from an offshoot of the ruling house who, like a remnant of the people according to Isa.6.13, will survive the catastrophe' (Kellermann, 24). However, it is wrong to talk of a 'son of David', as the tree of David will be cut down and all that will be left will be the 'root of Jesse'.

34. 'At all events, these expectations include a devastating judgment on the contemporary ruling house of David. Anyone who sees salvation so decisively embodied in the anointed one that is to come is saying that the contemporary house of David has lost its saving function which was so emphatically attributed to it in the royal psalms' (von Rad, 177). This should be stressed over against an over-hasty inclusion of this passage in 'the Israelite and even the general Near Eastern ideology of kingship' (Kaiser, 258). It makes a considerable difference whether such statements are made about actual reality or in the face of it.

35. The Hebrew text which has come down to us has *'ereṣ* (LXX γῆ) here, but the following line in parallel suggests that this should be seen as a mishearing of *'ārîṣ*.

36. For this text see Ebach, *Ursprung*, 77f., and for the whole context Isa.11.1-10, ibid., 75-89.

37. Kellermann stresses that here 'there is no warlike feature in the messianic hope. The theme of military power is transformed into the power of the word of judgment' (25).

38. According to Kaiser, ad loc., 'the coming king from the line of Jesse is to share God's capacity to see things and to decide on them as they really are' (127). We should not, however, understand this to mean that the messiah has a neutral position beyond or above the conflicts. He gets this picture of how 'things really are' by looking them from the perspective of the impoverished and the humiliated.

39. Cf. Ebach, 'Recht', 20: 'That the earliest texts of the Hebrew Bible already stress the rights of the poor (what is due them and not what is condescendingly granted them) means that they see the poor as brothers of equal value and with equal rights, not as the object of compassion. At the same time biblical texts stress that it is a question of specific help, indeed of economic and political change leading to a condition in which there are no longer any poor. How easily can this aim can be lost sight of? That happens, for example, where in a mistaken

interpretation of biblical texts which speak of a particular relationship between God and the poor poverty is given an aura of religious glorification.'

40. For the almost universal dating of Zephaniah's ministry under Josiah (639-609 BC) and indeed before 622 (cultic reform by the king), probably even before 630 (period of the king's minority; cf. Zeph.1.8), cf. Weiser, *Introduction*, 264; Rudolph, *Micah*, etc., 255.

41. Thus aptly Hempel, 323 n.4. Here he uses a phrase which was common in the sixteenth and seventeenth century; cf. 'HANS 1a', in *Deutsches Wörterbuch von Jacob Grimm und Wilhelm Grimm*, IV 2, Leipzig 1877, 456f. (with many examples, including Luther).

42. Thus Elliger, 80. Rudolph, *Micha*, etc., 297, writes on v.12: 'It emerges from the contrast with 11b that "poor and insignificant" here are not social but religious terms.' This is to overlook the fact that v.11b is also to be understood in social terms in so far as it has in mind the upper class, so that Rudolph has to translate *'ny* as *'nw* and finally assert without any support that *dal* 'here is not meant in an objective but a subjective sense: feeling small, thinking oneself small'. For the twofold aspect of 2.12 (social economic and ethical) cf. Schwantes, 151f.

43. The juxtaposition of πραΰς and ταπεινός is impossible in Greek ethics. The same thing is true of the Latin equivalents in the Roman sphere. Cf. above 7, 68 n.25. This parallelism occurs in Isa.26.6 as well as in Zephaniah. The whole section Isa.26.1-6 in any case has parallel content to Zeph.3.11-3: a people is to enter the city which God will have made secure who will show justice and faithfulness (vv.1f.). They will trust in God (v.4), who has cast down those who inhabited the high places, has hurled down the lofty city into the dust (v.5), 'that it is trodden under foot, the feet of the distressed (*'ānî*), the tread of the impoverished (*dallîm*)' (v.6) (LXX πόδες πραέων καὶ ταπεινῶν).

44. The invitation to the humble to show humility has constantly been felt offensive. Thus Elliger assumes 'that v.3a does not originally belong in this context' (69). But even if that were the case, an attempt would have to be made to understand the text in its present form. The solution by Rudolph, *Micha*, etc., 273f., is, however, misleading. He assumes that the comparative particle *k* has fallen out before *kl* by haplography, which produces as the text for v.3a: 'Seek Yahweh like all the humble of the land, who have practised his judgment...' This gives the following meaning to the section 2.1-3: those 'who as it were sit on their high horses in self-assurance and self-satisfaction' (273) – and these are (now I put the stress differently from Rudolph) 'the great Hanses', 'the godless upper classes' – shall become the same as those who are oppressed by them. The humility required of them - 'do what is just before God and the most important thing here is humility' (274) – is thus none other than giving up the oppression and exploitation that they practise. This leads to solidarity among the whole people of God.

45. According to Kraus the psalm is 'comparatively late, and at all events in the post-exilic period' (439).

46. Cf. esp.v.25.

47. The first two letters of each double verse are in alphabetical order (acrostic).

48. Vv.10, 12, 14, 16, 17, 20, 28, 34, 35, 38, 40.

49. Vv.2, 9, 10, 13, 15, 17, 20, 22, 28, 34, 35f.,38.

50. Vv.9, 11, 22, 29, 34.

51. Crüsemann cites Ps.37.25 as 'an example of the whole of earlier wisdom' (84). That is certainly right for the isolated verse. He sees it as the expression of the 'thought-form of a rich, landed upper class' (85) in which (it is formulated) as experience that 'normally a due degree of laziness, stupidity or behaviour deviating from social norms is an element in ending up in distress and downfall' (86). But the present context of this verse no longer expresses the perspective of the landed upper-class.

52. Vv. 3, 5, 7, 9, 34.

53. Vv. 12, 16,17,21, 25, 29, 30, 39.

54. On this passage Birkeland writes that 'here we seem to have an instance in which *'nwym* are completely synonymous with "pious"' (*ani*, 88f.). They are 'the wretched, the lost' (ibid., 92). They do not form a party, 'but the use of the word (must) be understood in terms of particularly historically conditioned factors' (ibid., 93). These are social factors. However, in a later work Birkeland thinks that there is a contrast in the psalms between Israel as 'the poor' and 'foreign enemies' (cf. the thesis in Feinde, 21f.). The wicked ones in Ps.37 are in his view 'the Gentiles who rule over Israel' (*Feinde*, 274; for Ps.37 see generally 273-5; cf. also id., *Evildoers*, 39ff.). One thing in Ps.37 which tells particularly against this theory is that the 'enemies' in v.38 are termed apostates; that cannot refer to Gentiles but must refer to Israelites. Against Birkeland cf. also Keel, 119.

55. On the connection between poverty and piety Dibelius observed: 'The more piety was understood as humbling oneself before God's will, the more poverty could function as intrinsically fertile soil for piety. As a result "poor" and "pious" appear as parallel concepts' (39). Over against this it should be stressed that the poor should in no way understand their situation as being in accordance with the will of God; 'humbling oneself before God's will' in no way means reconciling onself to the situation of oppression and exploitation. Poverty could become 'fertile soil for piety' in connection with the rich and their unjust methods. For 'poor' and 'humble' in the Psalms see also the excursus in Kraus, 82f.: 'A thorough investigation of the occurrence of the terms shows that the poor man is the one who is persecuted and without rights, who in the face of violent enemies... takes refuge with Yahweh and commends his lost cause to God as the just judge' (82).

56. For the dating Sacchi still thinks that here we have to rely on internal critria and sees 'no reason for departing from the usual date between the middle of the first century BC and the middle of the first century AD' (47). Over against this Uhlig and others are to be followed in their reference to Aramaic fragments found in Qumran which contain parts of the 'Epistle of Enoch'. According to Uhlig, 'round about the middle of the first century BC is the *terminus ante quem* for the earlier of the two Aramaic copies. However, we cannot rule out the possibility that some parts of the epistle were composed in the pre-Essene period' (Uhlig, 709). Hengel (II, 117f. n.460, with bibliography) argues that the whole work was written 'before about 150 BC'.

57. Nickelsburg, 'Message', 311.

58. Ibid., 318.

59. This is an independent revision of Jer.22.13. Cf. also 94.7: 'Woe to those who build their houses with sin'.

60. For the text cf. Nickelsburg, 'Riches', 329 and n.16.

61. For the conclusion cf. also 96.8; 'Woe to you, you powerful, who oppress the righteous with force!'

62. Nickelsburg, 'Message', 311.

63. 98.11; but cf. Gen.9.4; Lev.17.34; Deut.12.23; Acts 15.20,29.

64. 94.9; 95.2; 96.7.

65. 99.7; 104.9.

66. Cf our phrase 'have the shirt off his back'.

67. For the luxury of the rich cf. 98.2: 'You men put on more jewellery than women, and more multicoloured garments than a virgin. In sovereignty, in grandeur, and in authority, in silver, in gold, in clothing, in honour and in edibles, you spend money like water.' For the translation of the conclusion see Nickelsburg, 'Riches', 330.

68. See also 103.5c, 6 in comparison with Sirach 1.13, 18b; 11.26.

69. Cf. Prov.6.1-11.

70. Nickelsburg, 'Message', 318-22, has discovered a clear structure in 102.4-104.8: this part consists of four sections which relate to dead righteous, dead sinners, living righteous and living sinners. Each section is subdivided into three parts giving the address, the speech of the particular group and the answer of the author. This makes 103.9a also easily understandable: 'Do not say, you righteous and good, who are alive'. The reading adopted by Uhlig ('Do not say about the righteous and good who were alive') has the following speech spoken by the rich sinners, who put it 'ironically on to the lips of the pious' (738 n.a, on v.9). That seems artificial and hardly makes sense. Unfortunately Uhlig does not go into the convincing suggestion made by Nickelsburg.

71. According to Nickelsburg this is 'an imitation of words and expressions from Deut.28. The speakers affirm that they, the righteous, are experiencing the curses of the covenant. Instead of receiving a reward for righteousness they are suffering the evil that God has threatened upon sinners, and moreover they suffer this evil at the hand of the sinners' ('Message', 322). According to Ruppert this passage is 'not a dogmatic tractate on the necessity of the suffering of the righteous but an *outcry of the pious* from the oppression that they experience' (154). He regards it as 'a reflection of the bloody persecution of the Pharisees under Alexander Jannaeus (88-86 BC)' (155, cf. also 144).

72. The Hebrew phrase *šepal-rūaḥ* may underlie the conclusion of v.9, 'and our spirit is weak/small', in the sense of being humiliated; cf. Isa. 57.15.

73. Cf. Jub.1.16.

74. What King Agrippa commends in his 'peace speech' is a counsel from 'above'; 'Nothing stops the blows sooner than tolerating them with patience, and if the victim keeps still it leads to a transformation in the one afflicting him' (Josephus, *BJ* II,351). The admonitions of Jesus to offer the other cheek to the one who hits you and to give your cloak to the robber who takes your coat have

a different social context and a different intention (cf. Wengst, *Pax Romana*, 88-90).

75. Cf. 96.3 and a textual variant in 103.13; 'We looked to see whither we could fly before you in order to revive ourselves' (Uhlig, 738 n.13b).

76. Cf. 104.3, where the rulers are spoken of as the ones 'who assisted those who plundered you'.

77. It is incomprehensible how in the light of such statements Schottroff/ Stegemann can ask whether the conflict described here in Ethopian Enoch 94-104 'can be described as a social conflict at all' (45). They assert that 'The distress of the victims is not described as social distress but as political defeat' (ibid.). But the passage 103.9-15 throughout describes the social situation, the political ramifications of which are considered at the end.

78. Cf. 97.10.

79. Besides, in this short passage the threat of an annihilating judgment, of extermination, occurs very frequently.

80. Cf. 95.3; 96.1.

81. Cf. e.g. 96.8; 103.2-4: 'In the judgment the righteous receive what the sinners received in their lifetime and the sinners receive what they assume is the fate of the righteous' (Nickelsburg, 'Message', 320). Again it is incomprehensible how Schottroff/Stegemann should suppose that 'the hopes are not directed towards social equalization' (45).

82. Nickelsburg, 'Message', 326.

83. 'Woe unto you who write down false words and words of wickedness, for they write down their lies so that they are heard and forget the other.' Cf. also 99.1 and 104.10.

84. At this point reference should be made to the joint action organized by mothers and wives of those who have 'disappeared' in Latin America.

85. Cf. 97.3; 'What do you intend to do, you sinners? Whither will you flee on that day of judgment, when you hear the sound of the prayer of the righteous ones?' Cf. further 97.5. They will also hear their own 'unrighteous speeches' and 'your countenance will be covered with shame' (97.6). In Hermann Kasack's novel *Die Stadt hinter dem Strom* (The City beyond the River, Frankfurt 1964), the narrator describes how at one point in the city, which represents the intermediate state, there is 'a series of cages'. In each of them there was an enormous 'yellow gramophone horn from which a wild sound emerged. The people who crouched in solitary confinement in the cages tried to put their hands over their ears in order to avoid the sound from the horns.' This is the place where 'the demagogues, the state tyrants and the public speakers have to listen day in and day out to their own speeches, with which they once misled and stirred up their own people' (337).

86. It is worth recalling here the intercessions in the Confessing Church for those arrested under Nazi rule.

87. Cf. 98.14; 'Woe to you, who destroy the speech of the righteous'.

88. 95.3; 96.3; 102.4; 103.4; 104.6.

89. This is by far the most frequent designation of the group which stands over against the powerful rich.

90. The description of the wretched social situation in 103.9-15 is made out to be what 'the righteous' say.

91. Proverbs 30.14 is an exception: here it is said of a group of people: 'There are those whose teeth are swords, whose teeth are knives, to devour the poor from off the earth.' What is presented here in a relatively detached way (cf. also the context) is much more clearly focussed in a similar formulation in Hab.3.14, when it is said of God's action against such people: 'Thou didst pierce with thy shafts the head of his warriors, who came like a whirlwind to scatter me, rejoicing as if to devour the poor in secret.'

92. Cf.Sirach 1.27.

93. According to Plöger, 'humility' in 18.12 is to be understood as 'a sign of self-critical judgment' (213). Cf. also 11.2.

94. Cf. Plöger, 251: yir'at yhwh, following *anāwā asyndetically, is to be seen as an attribute: the reward of the humility founded on the fear of Yahweh.

95. For the circumstances of its composition (it was probably written in Jerusalem around 190 BC), cf. Sauer, 488-90; Hengel, I, 131-52.

96. Cf. also 10.14f.; 11.4f.

97. Literally: 'In your riches you shall walk in humility.'

98. Cf. also 10.28.

99. There is no sign of anxiety over the curse of the oppressed in Koheleth: 'Do not give heed to all the things that men say, lest you hear your servant cursing you' (7.21). – It is also clear from Sirach 7.32 to what extent concern for the poor is aimed at securing personal well-being: 'Stretch forth your hand to the poor, so that your blessing may be complete.'

100. Cf. also the further critical comments in vv.20-22.

101. Cf. Grundmann, 12.

102. The translation 'when your feet sink' is uncertain: Lohse puts a question mark here. Cf. also Jeremias, 226 nn.8, 9. However, we may be sure that this is meant to be the description of a situation of distress.

103. For the 'teacher of righteousness' cf. Jeremias, *Lehrer der Gerechtigkeit*, and on this psalm 226-44.

104. for this section of the psalm see Jeremias, 24f., and for the whole psalm Lichtenberger, 61-6. There is a parallel to the content in 1QH II, 32-35: 'And from the congregation of those who seek smooth things, thou hast redeemed the life of the poor one (*'ebyōn*) whom they planned to destroy, by spilling his blood because he served thee... But Thou, O my God, hast succoured the soul of the poor and the needy (*'ānī wārāš*) against one stronger than he.'

105. For the origin of the Qumran community cf. primarily H.Stegemann, *Die Enstehung der Qumrangemeinde*, esp. 198-252.

106. Cf. Jeremias. 36-78; Stegemann, 95-115.

107. Cf. 4QpPs 37 IV 8. Elliger stresses on 1QpHab XII, 'that the *'ebyōnīm* always appear without the article; so the word is a designation for a more or less clearly defined group but not a techical term, not a name' (87; cf.222). The passages from 4QpPs 37 make it clear, however, that this is the self-designation of a group and not the 'wider circle' of those from whom the group is recruited.

108. Cf. 4QpPs 37 passim; for the exegesis of Ps.37.8-11 in II 1-11 cf. Lichtenberger, 156-8.

109 . This aspect of the disguise is misunderstood by Awerbuch, 462.30, when in this and the passage I shall go on to mention she recognizes 'the demand for complete self-denial'. The 'self-denial' is merely the means compelled by the circumstance to keep one's own identity.

110. The Qumran community has a hierarchical division; cf. 1QS II 19-26, and in connection with the passages I have just quoted v.2 and above all vv.23f. As a result of this structure humility may in fact have continually assumed the forms of condescension and subservience. Careful attention should be paid to an instructive survey of the problem of the 'piety of the poor' in the Old Testament and Judaism, giving the basic details, in Lohfink.

IV. *'...and exalts the humble.' God's option for 'humility' in the primitive Christian tradition*

1. I shall not discuss here whether or not these verses originally belong with those which precede them, and start from what according to Wilckens, σοφία, 17 n.357, is almost a consensus: 'The original independence of vv.28-30 is nowadays accepted almost everywhere.' Cf. also Strecker, 172f., and Gnilka, *Matthäusevangelium*, 432f., though there is no basis for his traditio-historical solution of vv.28-30 (433).

2. 385. However, Schlatter also interprets the text in direct association with 23.4, and thus refers talk of the yoke and the burden to the law. For this widespread interpretation cf. the second paragraph of the following excursus.

3. For a literal understanding of Matt.11.28-30, cf. also Berger, 127.

4. Bammel, 908.

5. 45. Cf. also Percy, 110: 'It seems to me most probable... that this logion has in mind those who are oppressed by the burden of laborious work: to them Jesus give refreshment through his yoke, the yoke of the kingdom of God which he proclaims with his gift and his demands, and this helps them also to bear their earthly burdens.'

6. Cf. Schweizer, *Matthew*, 177: 'The "yoke" should probably be pictured not just as the ordinary yoke that a labourer lays across his shoulders with containers at both ends, but as the yoke imposed by the victor on the vanquished.' Arvdson, 174; 'Presumably at all times and in all parts of the world it has been natural to use the yoke as an image of servitude.' In connection with the burden see also Dio Chrysostom 34,41, who writes in connection with the Roman rule which is embodied in the governor: 'I think that this is like a burden. If it is too oppressive and we can no longer bear it, we seek to throw it off as quickly as possible; but if our burden is moderate and we see the need to carry either this or a greater burden, then we see that it is as light as possible. That is the case with a reasonable citizenship.'

7. See above, 27.

8. Volk, 161f.

9. Ibid., 162.

10. Cf. e.g. Grundmann, *Matthäus*, 317: 'All those who labour and bear burdens are invited. These include those who suffer from the manipulation of the law by the scribes.'

11. 'Almost all scholars are agreed that those who are invited in Matt.23.4 = Luke 11.46 are to be interpreted as those who suffer under the burden of the Pharisaic accentuation of the law' (Christ, 111).

12. For the comparison with Sirach 6 and 51 see the summaries in Christ, 12f., according to whom 'we may take it that a recollection of Sirach is probable'. Despite this scanty conclusion he goes on to say: 'So Jesus identifies himself with Ben Sirach's wisdom of God' (113).

13. Volk, 161f. Even in the book of Sirach, 'yoke' does not directly mean the law. In 40.1 it is a general description of human destiny. There is the absolute use of the 'yoke' in connection with the law in Aboth VI 6; SifDev § 93.

14. That cannot be said with the same certainty for the level of the Gospel of Matthew; according to Schottroff, 'Volk', 162, 'Matt.11.28f. (may)... also mean those who bear the burden of Pharisaic claims to rule.' This is supported not only by Matt.23.4 but also by the subsequent context in 12.1-14, which shows Jesus in conflicts over the sabbath.

15. In view of the new commentary on the Gospel of Matthew by Gnilka it must be stressed that here *only* 'those who torment and oppress themselves' are oppressed. Gnilka says: 'The great invitation is addressed to all, especially to the weary and heavy laden' (439; he already makes a very similar comment on 432).

16. Cf. 19 above and 74 n.25; also Dihle, who in connection with the account of the 'ideal of the cosmopolis' (739) which develops in philosophical ethics comments: 'However, this progressive view of equal rights for all human beings (at least in theory) does not come about through a demand for the exalted to diminish themselves and the self-aware to gain ground... It is no coincidence that words like ἡσιότης, ἐπιείκεια, *clementia, comitas* have long described particularly those qualities which are required of the ruler who, in full awareness of his power and status, condescends in a friendly way but does not humiliate himself' (740).

17. Thus, however, Klostermann 104. There is hardly any régime which does not feel itself to be humane.

18. Cf. above, 21f. and 76 n.43.

19. The comment by Christ, 116, 'The gentleness of Jesus best befits Jesus as wisdom', is a slick exaggeration. On the contrary, characterization of the speaker as πραῢς καὶ ταπεινὸς τῇ καρδίᾳ rules out an interpretation in terms of wisdom which Christ, 115f., obtains only in an artificial way.

20. Cf. Schlatter, 387: 'Taken by itself ταπεινός does not describe a modesty of the will but the state of powerlessness which is produced by restrictions on one's mode of life. Therefore τῇ καρδίᾳ is added to ταπεινός so that this limitation and constriction not only arises as a compulsion from outside as the result of a lack of means of power but is affirmed internally and deliberately described.' Cf. further Grundmann, ταπεινός, 20f. The phrase also occurs in the Septuagint addition Dan.3.87; εὐλογεῖτε, ὅσιοι καὶ ταπεινοὶ τῇ καρδίᾳ, τὸν κύριον. For the combination of πραῢς and ταπεινός or the equivalents in Judaism cf. Grundmann, 14.

21. Cf. Wengst, *Pax Romana*, 55-71.

22. Ethiopian Enoch 103.13, see 28 above.

23. According to Christ 'the imperative "Take my yoke upon you" immediately recalls wisdom' (109). Apart from the similarity in form he cites as a reason; 'Above all the twofold significance of the phrase "my yoke" can only be explained in the light of the wisdom tradition: "my yoke" is at the same time both the yoke that Jesus is and the yoke that Jesus imposes' (ibid.). This argument, however, is based on the presupposition that 'yoke' is to be understood as 'law' and Jesus as 'the new law' (107).

24. Cf. Schottroff, 'Volk', 161: 'His yoke is the end of being under the yoke'.

25. χρηστός is admirably translated at this point with Luther's archaic German word 'sanft', 'gentle'. Nowadays a precise rendering can be given only in a negative way. Thus Jens translates 'not hard' (46).

26. Literally 'for your souls'. However, the way in which those who are addressed are described, in terms which so clearly reflect the real world of work, makes it clear that here this is no abstract 'salvation of souls' – Rehrl, *Problem*, 177, speaks of 'rest for souls'. 'For your souls' means the human person and can be rendered 'for you' (Grundmann, *Matthäus*, 318). ψυχή here corresponds to *nepeš* as a designation of the person. This assumption sems all the more likely since there is a quotation from Jer.6.16. Cf. Jacob, 616f.; Schweizer, ψυχή, 638.

27. Cf. Ethiopian Enoch 103.13 and on it 28 above. What does not seem attainable, namely to find rest, is gained by following Jesus.

28. Thus Weiss, 86f., who then thinks that 'the specific signification of the term πεφορτισμένος is to be gathered from the contrast with the φορτία imposed by the rabbis. The reference is to those who sigh under rabbinic legal praxis' (87).

29. The Hebrew text and the Septuagint differ from each other at one point. The latter has ἁγνισμός ('purification') instead of ἀνάπαυσις ('rest'). Matt.11.29 thus corresponds to the Hebrew text. The logion therefore may not have arisen in the Greek sphere, but in an Aramaic Hebrew one. That stresses the possibility of a derivation from Jesus himself.

30. Weiser, 56.

31. Cf. Sirach 24.19: 'Come to me, you who desire me, and be filled with my fruits!' For further parallels cf. Christ, 103 and n.295.

32. For its Old Testament presuppositions and rabbinic parallels cf. Grundmann, ταπεινός, 8f., 14, 24-36.

33. Grundmann thinks it 'likely that we have here the meaning Jesus attached to the common saying', namely 'to become a child again before God, i.e. to trust him utterly, to expect everything from him and nothing from self' (ταπεινός, 17: cf. id., *Matthäus*, 414). However, his argument is no basis for this judgment. For he has to attribute precisely the words 'like this child' which distinguish Matt.18.4 to the Matthaean redaction because of the context.

34. 'The motivation is not high-flown morality but practical' (Schneider, 314). It is also above all tactical.

35. Suggestions for the origins of the Magnificat extend from the transposition of a Maccabaean psalm to a Lucan composition: cf. the brief information and bibliography in Schneider, 54-6. That Luke cannot be the author of the Magnificat is demonstrated by Farris, 14-30, and Schottroff, 'Magnificat', 304-6. See this article for the whole question.

36. Cf. Schürmann, 73f.: 'The ταπείνωσις... is simply to be understood as an expression of humility on the part of the handmaid of the Lord.' But he immediately adds; 'Here the situation of a girl in a lowly social position who is so far unknown may have had an intensifying effect.'

37. 'The lowliness is that of the maid over against the mighty (v.49) and in comparison to the mighty (v.52)' (Schneider, 57).

38. For a definition of the relationship between the two parts cf. Schottroff, 'Magnificat', 301f.

39. It is not clear from Schürmann's exegesis why he thinks that those with ethical religious qualifications in v.51 are only *'apparently* characterized in a political and social way in vv.52f.' (my italics). Certainly he guards against a domination of the statements by 'thinking in terms of human classes', but he does say that 'God must change the circumstances in the world if God's order is to arise' and that the revolution coming from God will also be a political and a social one' (76).

40. Cf. Grundmann, ταπεινός, 19: 'ὁ δὲ πλούσιος in the continuation defines ὁ ἀδελφὸς ὁ ταπεινός as the brother bowed down by poverty, the *ānī*.'

41. Thus Mussner, 74; however, one may not argue from the formal possibility of such an understanding directly to its necessity.

42. Cf. Dibelius, 117f., who sums up: 'Therefore, he may have had in mind primarily non-Christians; but if he was thinking here of Christians as well, then these are people whom he considers no longer to be included in a proper sense within Christianity.'

43. James 2.6f.; 5.1-6.

44. Cf. 4.13-17.

45. Dibelius, 84 (with examples).

46. Thus Mussner, who then adds the eschatological understanding by way of supplement. The future statements in vv.10,11 – 'he will pass away', 'he will disappear' – explain the ταπείνωσις mentioned earlier. So this envisages an event and not a state. Therefore the antithetical terms ὕψος and ταπείνωσις may not be translated 'height' and 'humility', as Mussner would want, but 'exaltation' and 'humiliation'.

47. Thus above all Dibelius, 85f. Schrage, *Jakobusbrief*, 18, is undecided: however, Mussner, 74, argues for an authentic paraenesis to the rich members of the community which is meant seriously, and Bultmann, 652, paraphrases v.10a out of context: 'that he humbles himself and glories in God alone'.

48. The continuation of the text makes it clear that the 'reward crying to heaven is none other than the cry of the harvesters themselves calling for the vengeance of God' (Mussner, 196). For modern analogies to the withholding of wages see Günther Wallraff, *Ganz unten*, Cologne 1985; cf. especially the case of S, 127-31.

49. As in the Old Testament-Jewish tradition discussed above, here, too, the humiliated poor man is 'the righteous' man. Verse 6 ends with the statement that the righteous man 'does not resist you'. Here probably what is envisaged is 'simply actual defencelessness in contrast to the brutal power of the rich' (Schrage, *Jakobusbrief*, 52).

50. The phenomena enumerated here should 'recall less the transitoriness of

earthly riches than the merciless, unsocial conduct of the rich' (Schrage, *Jakobusbrief*, 51).

51. For the possible ways of understanding the phrase 'on the day of slaughter' cf. Schrage, *Jakobusbrief*, 51f.

52. The rich 'oppress, criminalize and taunt the community' (Burchard, 324). Given the economic and social background which is evident in the Letter of James it is strange that Mussner wants to see the rich as the Jews who 'were the particular opponents of the young church' (81f.; the quotation on 81, cf. also 122, 198).

53. Cf. Burchard, 322-5.

54. Mussner, 179: he makes it probable that φονεύετε (you kill) must not be conjectured as an emendation for φθονεῖτε (you are envious) but can be understood with ζηλοῦτε (you are zealous) along the lines of the quotation above (178).

55. According to Burchard unity is the *notissima nota ecclesiae* (321).

56. For 2.15f. see the illuminating explanations by Burchard, 325f.

57. Cf. Grundmann, ταπεινός, 20: 'servile, abject, ineffectual, inferior'. Rehrl, *Problem*, 175: 'spiritless, cowardly, abashed'.

58. 'At the least [the reproach] is based on the fact that during his last stay Paul had not been able to control the community, but had had to let even the insult mentioned in chs.2 and 7 go by him and left without returning, as he had first envisaged' (Lietzmann, 140). For the literary criticism of II Corinthians and the course of events I refer here only to Vielhauer, 143-5, without agreeing with all the details of the hypotheses outlined there.

59. II Cor.2.5; 7.12.

60. All those who feel the need for literary-critical operations on II Corinthians agree that the 'conciliatory letter' to which this passage belongs comes later in time than the 'tearful letter' (chs.10-13).

61. Against Dihle, 750.

62. Cf. Giesen, 803: 'live in deprivation'.

63. When it comes to the 'abundance', however, we should note with Schrage that 'Paul generally led a life of self-denial' (*Ethics*, 221).

64. See above, 5f., 7f.

65. Cf. also the passage with parallel content, I Cor.9.19, where in connection with his manual work Paul speaks of his slavery. For the question of the social position of Paul in respect of both passages cf. Hock, passim; further Wengst, *Pax Romana*, 75.

66. To this degree we are to agree with Hock when he writes that the language of Paul in these passages reflects 'the snobbish and contemptuous attitude to manual work which is so typical of upper-class Greeks and Romans' (562; cf. 560). But that is only half the matter.

67. Cf. I Cor.9.

68. Of course, τοῖς ταπεινοῖς can also be understood as neuter; in that case it would be in strict antithetical parallel to τὰ ὑψηλά. Schlier, *Römerbrief*, 380f., argues for this; he interprets the verse as an admonition to forgo high office and pre-eminence. Both possibilites are left open by Wilckens, *Römer* 3, 23 n.113; Grundmann, ταπεινός, 20. The latter explains the neuter in this way: 'Paul has

in mind the small and insignificant services by which the one can help the other' (20). However, as the weak above all need these services, here the focus is basically on 'the lowly'. In the light of the immediate context – unanimity, not being wise for oneself – what is intended is probably a contrast between a concern for upward mobility and solidarity with the worse-off. For a masculine understanding of τοῖς ταπεινοῖς cf. also Giesen, 799; Käsemann, *Romans*, 348, according to whom the point here is that 'fellowship with the lowly and oppressed must be maintained'.

69. Cf. Wilckens, *Römer*, 3,23: 'As a Christian one can only be reasonable if one is reasonable over others.'

70. Käsemann, *Romans*, 348, concludes from this passage: 'What is now called fellow-humanity is unalterably connected with the fact that the community of Jesus is able to stand on the side of the lowly and also to break through the class ghetto.'

71. Wilckens, *Römer* 3, 17, translates this very well: 'Where the saints are in need, share with them!'

72. He introduces it in the form of a ἵνα statement.

73 For the Christ-hymn in Phil.2.6-11 see Gnilka, *Philipperbrief*, 31-47.

74. It is hardly appropriate to translate παράκλησις with only one word here. For παρακαλεῖν/παράκλησις in Paul see the detailed study in Schlier, *Eigenart*, passim.

75. Cf. Käsemann, 'Analyse', 90f.

76. That is certainly 'a demand for collective humility' which cannot be dismissed as 'absurd', as Radler does with his stress on humility as an 'individual-ethical factor' (486). He does not consider the community as an ethical subject. Dihle offers an individualizing exegesis of Phil.2.3 which does not perceive the community dimension: 'ταπείνωσις or ταπεινοφροσύνη towards the neighbour is the only appropriate behaviour for the one whom God encounters in the neighbour, for whom all men are sinners without rights, fallen and forgiven, who have no claims to make' (749).

77. Cf. above 8-10.

78. The category of renunciation determines the interpretation by Rehrl, *Demut*, 64f., very strongly.

79. 324; similarly in the summary, 326. Earlier he had mentioned not only bravery but also 'loyalty to one master' as an important factor in upward mobility (321), together with relevant examples (322-4), and stressed the way in which the two factors belong together (325).

80. At least it is impossible to talk sweepingly of 'loyalty in ascent for all' (326) and 'each' (324). According to I Cor.1.27f., the election of the foolish, the weak and the ignoble by God puts the wise and the strong to shame, and destroys anything worth anything. Granted, according to I Cor.7.22 the slave chosen in the Lord is a freeman of Christ, but the freeman who is chosen is a slave of Christ. Each has the experience of the other: if one likes to put it that way – one of rise, another of fall. Naturally for Paul 'slave of Christ' is a 'higher' designation than 'free man', but since he uses the social terms in so varied a way it does not seem to me to be appropriate to speak of 'loyalty in ascent for all'.

81. Thus 'to regard something as robbery' is probably the best translation.

For ἁρπαγμόν τι ἡγεῖσθαι and related phrases cf. Foerster, 472f.; for discussion of the interpretation of v.6 see Gnilka, *Philipperbrief*, 15-17.

82. Hofius, 61; cf. 58, where he rightly stresses that the significance of the expressions 'form of God' and 'servant of God' must be inferred from the formulation of the Christ-hymn itself.

83. Theissen, 325.

84. Cf.Hofius, 59f.

85. Against the widespread thesis that here 'humanity is understood as slavery' (thus e.g. Gnilka, *Philipperbrief*, 120), cf. Hofius, 62f.

86. ὑπήκοος is usually translated 'obedient' here. But there is no mention nor even a hint of any instruction or a divine plan which Christ follows in obedience, nor is it even hinted at. It is not enough for Hofius to say: 'Neither linguistically nor in terms of content does the stress in this sentence lie on the word "obedient" but on the terminus "until death"' (63); finally, the word ὑπήκοος cannot simply be ignored in the interpretation. It is completely in keeping with the pattern of the hymn and makes a meaningful extension of the saying about self-humiliation if it is understood as a literal rendering of the word 'slave' in terms of being 'subject', 'subservient' (cf. Plutarch, *Moralia* 234c; Rom.6.16). The new aspect of this passage lies in the stress on obedience until death, i.e. lifelong helplessness.

87. The phrase 'even to the death of the cross' in v.8c is usually understood as a Pauline addition to an existing hymn. In a thorough criticism of this assumption Hofius has shown that it is not tenable (3-17). 'The word σταυρός standing so emphatically at the end of the first strophe provides the most striking contrast to the words ἐν μορφῇ θεοῦ ὑπάρχων with which the first line of the hymn begins' (12). 'To such a degree has the one equal to God assumed the form of a slave that he even took upon himself the *servitutis extremum summumque supplicium*, the *mors turpissima crucis*' (16; the quotations are from Cicero, *Verr.* 2, 5, 66 [§ 169]; Origen, *Matth.comm.ser.*124). 'The fact of his death on the cross may be the starting point for the description in this hymn of Christ, who was no slave, as a slave. The word here is 'to be understood as a metaphor for that helplessness and shame in which Christ surrendered himself, renouncing his divine power and glory' (Hofius, 61).

88. Pliny, *Panegyricus*, 71.1, 4f.; cf. also the quotation from 4.5 on 11 above.

89. All the inhabitants of the world, which is imagined here as having three storeys, acclaim Jesus Christ as the Lord. It is impossible to decide whether this acclamation is future or present. If it is present, here as in Rev.5.13 we have an anticipation. At all events, this acclamation describes God's purpose for the world.

90. Domitian was certainly the first to have himself addressed as 'Lord and God', but in the east of the empire Augustus was already venerated as a god – coupled with the goddess Roma. By calling himself *divi filius*, he also surrounded himself with a divine aura. For the religious veneration of the emperor cf. Wengst, *Pax*, 47-50.

91. For examples from antiquity see Dio Cassius 54,23, 1f.; Pliny, *Epistles* III,14,1.

92. Cf. Mehl 81: 'Therefore God is concerned to seek out his creature, to

become his neighbour in Christ Jesus. Here is the touchstone of all true humility, the point at which it radically parts company with all condescension with which arrogance can feel easy.'

93. Cf. also Col.3.15.

94. Lohse, 213.

95. There is quite a different use of 'humility' in Col.2.18, 23, where the author is refering to remarks made by the heretics with whom he is in conflict. There humility at one point stands alongside 'service of the angels' and at another alongside 'voluntary service' and 'strict control of the body'. It occurs in the context of the worship of the powers in Colossian philosophy which is expressed in cultic practices (2.17), the observation of tabus (2.21) and in asceticism (2.23). 'Humility' here is submission to the power of oppression as a means of participating in it; cf. Wengst, 'Versöhnung', 15f.

96. Cf. Schnackenburg, 165: the author is writing about 'the unity which is given by God to the church beforehand but which is the constant task of all Christians'.

97. Eph.4.4-6; esp.v.5: 'One Lord, one faith, one baptism'.

98. Eph.4.13-16.

99. Cf. Schlier, *Epheser*, 171: 'ταπεινοφροσύνη is the disposition and the conduct of those who think more of others than of themselves, and do so not in order to lord it over them but out of a real modesty which recognizes that which is given by God to the others and to themselves for what it is.' However, Schlier's view that the remarks in I Clement are a 'commentary on this passage' is a mistaken one, cf. below section 3.

100. Cf. also I Peter 3.8f.

101. According to Brox, this ethic moves 'on the razor's edge between the real success of mutuality... and decadence leading to a trivial regulatory morality' (235).

102. For introductory questions cf. Vielhauer, 530-40.

103. Cf. Brunner, 130-5.

104. Does this not already show a typical Roman perspective? For the peoples had to behave as *subiecti* towards Rome; cf. just Virgil, *Aeneid*, 6, 853.

105. Brunner notes that 'the author approaches humility in terms of obedience' (13).

106. 13.1; cf. 2.1.

107. The example of Moses presented in 17.5, read in its Old Testament context Ex.3f., is more the counterpart of a model of obedience.

108. It should be noted that 'outbursts of a revolutionary disposition' can be a burden only for those who are established in a particular system and profit from it.

109. Of course Clement is not making any contrast here between admonishing the Roman community and the will of God, but the latter already appears in the former; that is what the 'rebels' have to recognize.

110. Cf. Brunner, 128-34; according to him 'humility has become an attitude related to authority' (133); it is 'in particular the attitude of obedient integration and subordination' (ibid.), 'the attitude which recognizes religious authority for its own sake' (134).

111. However, Brunner comments: 'Without exception he (i.e. I Clement) takes up only the biblical Jewish tradition and here only the positive religious tradition and develops it' (132).

112. Cf. the quotation from Prov.3.34 in 30.2.

113. For the geographical and social setting cf. Wengst, *Pax Romana*, 135f.

V.　*Conclusion: '...among the crosses of the oppressed'*

1. Heinrich Heine, *Die romantische Schule* (1835), Sämtliche Schriften 5, Reihe Hanser 220/5, Munich and Vienna 1976, (357-504) 362.

2. Takatso A.Mofokeng, *The Crucified Among the Crossbearers. Towards a Black Christology*, Kampen 1983.

3. The black community 'recovers, reappropriates its entire negative history and cultural heritage, i.e. a negative blackness, and accepts it, becoming a comprehensive black subject that utilizes black negativity for liberation' (43). 'The victims of human injustice are freed from a negative view of themselves by the Son of God's identification and solidarity, which he does by taking their being and condition upon himself' (258).

4. Cf.263: 'The Son lives never to die again and raises a community that loves and suffers with Him, struggling against the powers of contradiction to the liberation of man and for the emergence of a new world with justice for the dispossessed and fraternity among man.'

5. Reiner Kunze, *Auf eigene hoffnung*, Frankfurt am Main ²1981, 38.

6. G.Gutierrez, *The Power of the Poor in History*, Orbis Books and SCM Press 1983, 140.

Index

(a) Old Testament and Judaism

(b) Greek and Roman Writers

(c) Primitive Christianity and the Early Church

Index

DATE DUE

HIGHSMITH   #LO-45220